Architecture Canada 1999

Tuns Press
Faculty of Architecture
Dalhousie University
P.O. Box 1000
Halifax, Nova Scotia
Canada B3J 2X4
URL: tunspress.dal.ca

General Editor: Essy Baniassad
Managing Director: Donald Westin

Distributed in the United Kingdom and Europe by:
Cardiff Academic Press, St. Fagans Road,
Fairwater, Cardiff CF5 3AE, United Kingdom

Editor: Essy Baniassad
Design: Hahn Smith Design
Designers: SMALL/Andrew Di Rosa & Andrew Kim
Text Editor: Stephen Parcell
Traductrice: Michèle Lejars
Réviseure: Nicole Larivée-Parenteau
Editorial Assistant: Judy Scott
Production: Donald Westin
Printing: Friesens

National Library of Canada Cataloguing Data
Architecture Canada (Ottawa, Ont.)
    Architecture Canada

    Biennial.
    Published: Halifax, N.S., 1997-
    Includes some text in French.
    Continues: Governor General's awards for architecture 1189-6388.
    ISSN 1209-7136
    ISBN 0-929112-45-8 (1999)

1. Governor General's Medals for Architecture. 2. Architecture, Modern –
20th century – Canada. 3. Architecture – Awards – Canada.

NA2345.C3G68   720'.79'71   C97-390075-X

Sponsors:
Gold/Or: The McGraw-Hill Construction Information Group
Silver/Argent: Hanscomb Ltd.
Bronze: DPIC (Security Insurance of Hartford);
Gage-Babcock & Associates Ltd.;
R.A. Duff & Associates Inc.;
Read Jones Christoffersen Ltd.;
Rheinzink Canada Ltd.

Sweet's Group • F.W.DODGE
McGraw-Hill Construction Information Group
A Division of The McGraw-Hill Companies

Hanscomb

The Canada Council
Conseil des Arts du Canada

Architecture Canada 1999

The Governor General's Medals for Architecture / Les Médailles du gouverneur général pour l'architecture

Edited by / Sous la direction de

Essy Baniassad

Contents

Foreword

Architecture is about more than how buildings and cities look; it is about how we live and how we feel about where we live. Issues such as style, function, efficiency, accessibility and environment affect the shape of our homes, communities and cities, and how much we enjoy them. Architects must consider these issues every day. What they decide, and the clarity of their vision, affects all of us.

Their decisions reveal the people, the values and the social conditions that have contributed to building a nation. The architecture of the country is reflected in office complexes and sports and cultural centres, and in our houses and homes for the aged. Canadian architecture is indeed an integral part of our lives and of the social and cultural landscape of our country.

The Governor General's Medals for Architecture recognize the imagination, talent and sophistication of Canadian architects, as well as their contributions to our country. I congratulate all the recipients of the 1999 Governor General's Medals. Your vision is helping to build this country, and I offer you my best wishes for continued success in the future.

Roméo LeBlanc
Governor General of Canada
May 1999

Preface

The Governor General's Medals for Architecture serve to recognize outstanding achievement in Canadian architecture by Canadian architects. The awards fulfill a critical role in promoting excellence in the development of the built environment.

In looking back over the historical records and publications of the Governor General's program, one can see the emergence of important movements and individuals who have shaped Canadian architecture in recent decades and have thus contributed to our nation's heritage and culture through their accomplishments.

Upon completing its review, the jury determined that ten projects deserved formal recognition as winners in this year's competition. It was their judgement that these projects reflected two tiers of work, with five projects in each tier. The ten winners of the 1999 Governor General's Medals for Architecture received either a "Medal for Excellence" or a "Medal for Merit," depending on the jury's recommendation.

The Institute has been most pleased to collaborate with the Canada Council in this current competition, as it has since 1990. We would like to express our appreciation for the invaluable resources and advice that the Council has contributed. On behalf of the Board of Directors and the profession, I would also like to express our appreciation to those who agreed to sit on the jury, recognizing the generous commitment they have made to the profession in undertaking this role. Finally, I would like to extend our thanks to the sponsors of the 1999 Governor General's Medals for Architecture program, and in particular, to the McGraw-Hill Construction Information Group, our 1999 Governor General's Gold Sponsor.

Eva Matsuzaki, FRAIC
President, Royal Architectural Institute of Canada

Avant-propos

L'architecture, c'est beaucoup plus que l'aspect extérieur des immeubles et des villes –
c'est aussi le reflet de notre mode de vie et du sentiment de bien-être que nous éprouvons
par rapport à l'endroit où l'on vit. Des éléments tels que le style, la fonction, l'efficacité,
l'accessibilité et l'environnement déterminent la forme que prennent nos maisons, nos
communautés et nos villes et le plaisir que nous retirons à y vivre. Les architectes doivent
quotidiennement tenir compte de ces facteurs. Leurs disions à cet égard et la clarté de leur
vision ont un effet sur chacun de nous.

Leurs choix révèlent les personnes, les valeurs et les conditions sociales qui ont con-
tribué à l'édification de la nation. L'architecture du pays est reflétée dans les immeubles
de bureaux et les centres sportifs et culturels ainsi que dans nos maisons et résidences
pour personnes âgées. L'architecture canadienne fait véritablement partie intégrante de
nos vies et du paysage social et culturel de notre pays.

Les Médailles du gouverneur général pour l'architecture rendent hommage à l'imagination, au talent et au raffinement des architectes canadiens, de même qu'à leur contribution au pays. Je félicite tous les lauréats du concours de 1999 pour les Médailles du
Gouverneur général pour l'architecture. Votre vision aide à bâtir ce pays. Je vous souhaite
mes meilleurs voeux de succès pour l'avenir.

Roméo LeBlanc
Gouverneur général
Mai 1999

Préface

Les Médailles du gouverneur général pour l'architecture récompensent les accomplissements remarquables d'architectes canadiens. Elles jouent un rôle essentiel pour promouvoir l'excellence dans l'amélioration de l'environnement bâti.

L'examen des dossiers et des publications passées concernant le programme du Gouverneur général révèle l'émergence d'importants mouvements et de personnes qui ont façonné l'architecture canadienne dans les dernières décennies et qui ont ainsi enrichi le patrimoine et la culture de notre pays.

À l'issue du concours, le jury a déterminé que dix projets, répartis également en deux catégories, méritaient d'être récompensés officiellement cette année. Les dix lauréats des Médailles du gouverneur général pour l'architecture de 1999 ont reçu soit une « Médaille d'excellence », soit une « Médaille du mérite », selon la recommandation du jury.

L'Institut a eu le grand plaisir de collaborer avec le Conseil des arts du Canada comme il le fait depuis 1990. Nous aimerions le remercier sincèrement pour les précieux conseils et les ressources qu'il nous a fournis. Au nom du conseil d'administration et de la profession, je tiens aussi à exprimer notre reconnaissance aux personnes qui ont accepté de faire partie du jury et ont ainsi apporté une généreuse contribution à la profession. Finalement, je remercie les commanditaires du programme des Médailles du gouverneur général pour l'architecture, et en particulier, le McGraw-Hill Construction Information Group, notre commanditaire Or de cette année.

Eva Matsuzaki, FRAIC
La Présidente, L'Institut Royal d'Architecture du Canada

On the Edge:

Remarks on the 1999 Governor General's Medals for Architecture

Wilfried Wang

In a global civilization that is still dominated by Anglo-Saxon culture and short term accountancy, it is not surprising to note the cautionary advice expressed particularly in those societies on the periphery of such a dominant culture. The cautionary advice is premised on the desire that such peripheral cultures should develop an identity of their own in order to resist such cultural hegemony. Such advice then precipitates a string of questions as to the nature of such an identity, its physical manifestation and compositional constitution, its relation to the material context, to tradition and to the ineradicable effects of modern social alienation and cultural abstraction – questions that, if seriously addressed, will undoubtedly refute the premise altogether. Such advice, if analyzed, will also reveal the origin of these concerns. It is formulated not so much in the fear of becoming yet another subsystem of the dominant culture – although this is an obvious moment in the countermoving force though frequently unsubstantiated in fact – but formulated more in the tradition of actualizing if not fashioning a rallying point for the populace in the face of an ever increasing rate of change in all parameters of a dominated culture.

Societies on the northernmost part of the globe, such as Scandinavia and Canada, are situated on the periphery of the dominant culture of the twentieth century, that of the United States of America. During the previous two centuries the Mediterranean cultures of France, Italy and Greece were the idealized foci. Caught between the art historiographically legitimated cultural realm of ancient Europe and the irresistible cultural osmosis with the American ideal, northern societies early this century sought architectural refuge in a national romance with a Richardsonian pensiveness. Ottawa's official architecture, Stockholm's Town Hall and governmental buildings, and Helsinki's Railway Station all give evidence of this romance. In their assertion of a particular identity, time was to have been overcome, too. These national monuments transposed the stones of Venice to the north, adapting the fragile elements and materials from the mellow south to the harsh northern climates, thus making them resistant to steady if gradual degradation across centuries. At the end of the twentieth century, the national romanticist monuments from the beginning of the twentieth century are regarded as isolated bulwarks. Their scattering across a vast territory such as Canada merely references this earlier attempt as a peripatetic infusion for the purposes of stabilising a young territory. However, today's desire for an identity – at least in the way it is expressed in the speeches written for politicians – is not confined to such individual bulwarks, but to a collective environment and therefore to the dream of a homogeneous cultural landscape as idealized, for instance, in vernacular hillside villages.

Such a dream of a superficial homogeneity is perhaps the naïve counterpart to the fear of becoming a subsystem of a dominant culture. While underlying, structural parallels in the shaping of a given culture can be traced across the globe – taking, for example, the car as a major unifying element with its demands on various infrastructures – other ordering systems that have transcended time, such as property patterns that give rise to urban rhythms, can be a force in the formation of a distinct appearance of a settlement fabric. Toronto, Vancouver, and Montreal may each be influenced by the architecture and urbanism of the United States of America, yet these cities' historical property patterns guarantee distinctions. Certainly, given enough time, such rhythms may disappear in the course of the amalgamation of plots, the construction of highways or the closure of streets; in short, they may disappear as a result of globalizing pressures, but to date, such distinctions are still discernible.

Centre d'intérêt minier de Chibougamau

On another level, topographic conditions and the prevailing climate have in the past influenced the response of construction. In societies with limited resources, nature was a force to consider. Choices of site, materials and details were to be integrated with the prevailing wind and rain; transport distances and available craft skills had to be weighed. Today, nature's vicissitudes have mostly been overcome by human instruments and constructs. Great disasters such as storms and earthquakes are the few exceptions that still test man's primary line of defence: the built environment; but on the whole, comfort devices such as artificial lighting, heating and ventilation, sturdy or light weight construction, mechanical transportation devices, active and passive solar energy collectors, and so forth, have allowed man to build in the most inhospitable regions of the world. Often, nature is therefore regarded as a source of inspiration, or more generally, as a bucolic context to which an equally serene architecture could respond; or further, it is regarded as a state of balanced existence with which architecture should be integrated. All three attitudes clearly document the romantic relation to a nature considered benign, an ecological system which, because man believes that he has successfully brought it under his control, he thus feels assured enough to judge it as something harmless, something that no longer threatens his existence but instead offers a maternal envelope, protectively restitutive on the one hand and poetically inspirational on the other.

If, on the one hand, the extant built fabric from past centuries still offers some moment of cultural difference, and on the other hand, methods of construction, systems and mechanisms in the running of buildings have been devised with the aim of supporting an ever increasing level of comfort, then the distance from true nature is equally growing. True nature, with its as yet unpredictable, occasional catastrophic phenomena, coupled with man's own predictable gradual catastrophic influence on it, is suppressed as a reality. While it is true that earthquakes have led to reviews in the structural requirements of buildings in threatened zones, the gradual catastrophic influence of man's unlimited consumption of resources has not reversed the rate of built development nor significantly changed the manner of construction. True nature is indivisible, potentially life threatening and, up to now, uncontrollable. Were this to be taken as the premise on which to build even at this late stage in contemporary civilization, it could inspire clients and architects to curb their desires to erect monuments to their own vanity, it would reverse the rate of consumption in physical as well as aesthetic terms, and in terms of the general character of such an architecture that respects true nature, it could express with a palpable modesty the sublime physical and inspirational force of such an understood nature, indeed revealing man's dependence on it.

Architecture thus is an index of such a distance to true nature. It is a characterization of civilization's attitude towards dependence: dependence on the surroundings in every aspect, whether climate, society, or built fabric. Traditionally, architecture has been the symbol of resistance to nature's forces, bringing about the understanding of nature's forces through its very existence. In this sense, architecture acts as a mirror to nature, despite its existence in nature. Quite another attitude could be defined by the notion of complementarity to nature. This topoi encompasses a range of relations. From this vantage point, architecture can be considered as a fragile extension of man's most directly needed envelope. An envelope of such a persuasion would thus be merely a mediator, a prosthesis between human needs and nature's, perhaps even society's vicissitudes. In its final state, such an architecture would reveal its fragility and temporality as a mere ruin. Architecture in this sense is far from asserting perfection, purity, completeness; instead, it is closer to embracing human inadequacy, always mindful of the need for ingenuity to temporarily overcome such a deficit.

Aware of the finality of resources, the minimal in a complementary architecture would establish the fragile balance between the constancy of nature and the temporariness of human presence. Considering such a position, it becomes clear that the civilization of dominant Anglo-Saxon culture is the decoration of true wilderness, a civilization whose decor is gradually unmasking itself. The architecture of dominant Anglo-Saxon culture reveals such a barbarous face. A complementary architecture recognizes instead the uniqueness of the here and now. This could be one definition of identity.

Seeing the awards of the 1999 Governor General's Medals in this context, two objects in Toronto's Ledbury and Rotary Parks deal most directly with prevailing climate. It is not surprising that the client, the Parks and Recreation Department, engendered a stance in favour of the ease of long-term maintenance and a concern for the environmental impact of such buildings. Both interventions provide a public swimming pool, Ledbury Park additionally offering a wading pool or ice rink. In their urban contexts, both schemes echo the orthogonality of the surroundings, placing each L-shaped configuration on their respective sites so that intelligible open spaces are bounded or implied. The Rotary Park Pool goes so far as to preserve a copse of willows and elms to its south.

Considering the architectural composition of both structures, important differences in the way, for instance, such relatively minor elements as canopies or pergolae indicate the building's self-understanding and its relation to the context – whether thought of as landscape, as an artificial construct, or as nature – can be discerned. In the case of the Rotary Park Pool, the pergola elements develop, so to speak, from a cylindrical vertical cantilever that supports an eccentrically placed tapered steel I-section, in which joists are then fixed. Here, on the one hand, the formal parallel to a tree-trunk can be read, but also, on the other hand, the traditional tectonic order of primary and secondary structures. This pergola is closer to an architectural, that is to say, a trabeated formal logic than that at Ledbury Park. In the latter case, the vertical support is a cluster of equal angles that extends beyond the lower plane of trellis joists so that the tectonic connection is not immediately visible. From the main joist, all subsidiary elements are hung. As such, the entire composition can be read as a simile of vegetal structure rather than trabeation. The ensuing lightness of the Ledbury Park pergola is not echoed in the detailing of the roof canopy to the view pavilion. Here a plane of wooden panels creates a closed surface that stands in distinction to the vegetal interpretation of the pergola.

Given the categorization in the award between the Medal for Excellence and that for Merit, such differences in the detailing of the two park structures may indicate the qualitative grounds for such distinctions. Ledbury Park is, with the various contradictions that might be discernible in the formal exposition of the parts, an attempt at creating an artificial, hard landscape, or put in another way, it is architecture as landscape. Together with its subtle bridge, a cross between a Litzka and a glue-laminated beam structure – a somewhat extravagant (what is not extravagant in good architecture, and yet so necessary as a constituting cause of it?) element in the overall composition – Ledbury Park is a formal exploration in a different, less tried realm of architectural design.

On a more immediate level, through the simple placement of copper clad walls from the mouth of a mining tunnel to its interior – in order to discreetly reflect on the former use as copper mine, together with the laconic infill of the rail tracks with pine planks as the powerful continuity element; the thin red line, so to speak – a visitor to the Bruneau Mine Interpretive Centre at Chibougamau would be confronted with the mine's past. Chain link fencing to the soffit leaves the threat of collapse lingering. Simple additions of furniture items, racks, the curved corrugated copper welcome desk, a copper wash hand trough, and even the entrance gate allow for the former mine to take centre stage. While the copper clad wall serves as an important orienting device, complete with its recessed light fit-

Ledbury Park

ting on the upper edge, its panel-like construction, suggesting substance through visual gauge beyond the thickness of each individual panel, it is less direct constructionally than the other pieces. All the same, the spirit of the architect's intervention is praiseworthy, in the way that it achieves a balance between new use and the drama of man's primary intervention in nature.

Two further interventions within a pre-existing man-made condition are Strachan House and the Cinémathèque québécoise. Undoubtedly, one of the most important undertakings in contemporary architecture is the adaptive maintenance of the existing fabric, if the built environment and the building industry are understood as centrally involved with the management of resources (inherent energy, CO_2 emissions, etc.). If this is fused with the accommodation of chronically homeless, and on top of this, their active involvement in the planning and construction of their future homes, then expectations of high quality architecture might be prejudicially low. All the more respect is due to the remarkable conversion of a nineteenth century warehouse on the edge of Toronto's downtown.

In an eight year project, a convincing set of bedrooms and sleeping nooks, together with communal facilities, were installed in a spatial manner that provides an urban interior with clear transitional spaces that could be read as "streets" and gathering spaces, to which the architects refer as the agora or front porches of the respective houses. The condition that draws the homeless to the streets is the latter's offer of numerous escapes. Choice of movement and clear visibility along the curved routes within Strachan House were thus paramount, while avoiding the institutionalization of the building through straight corridors. The curved route assures the identity of each house. A system of porches and pergolae marks thresholds within the loft-like height of each warehouse floor space.

As such, the pervasive impression of the construction, using rough sawn timbers in combination with plywood and other smoothly finished sheet material, heightens the difference between an interiorized "street" environment, where the possibility of escape is needed, and the simultaneously required sense of shelter in the individual's domestic cell. The spatial explorations around the hallways, lounges and the "Town Hall" square are inventive in their accommodation of multiple forms of occupation and in their involvement of artists and craftsmen. Strachan House is an exemplary synthesis of a fundamental need realized in an entirely appropriate architecture, an architecture that has the users at the heart of its concern, and a concern that in turn celebrates the spirit of the undertaking in every detail.

The Cinémathèque québécoise in Montreal brings together two buildings by the insertion of an entrance volume with an additional cinema, video room and cafeteria. Rather

Strachan House

than filling the gap between the pre-existing masonry structures, the new building forms an outdoor space that brings light into the circulation areas, as well as forming a courtyard to the cafeteria. At the new centre of the cinémathèque complex is thus the main entrance, a generous hall that simultaneously acts as a projection space while providing clear orientation for the visitors. Such orientation is layered, almost episodic and multifaceted so that one never has a sense of being in a calculating institution.

The integration of new and old, on the inside and out, is brilliantly stated in front of the old school: here the steel footbridge on the upper level of the entrance volume on the one hand forms a screen and on the other hand supports a projection screen. The new plane brings the slightly set back school building to the fore, thereby aligning the two pre-existing buildings within a gradually receding building line. The intermingling of image and users, the central idea behind the architectural concept too, becomes the eidetic projection into the public domain. The new and the old fabrics are juxtaposed in an overlaid condensation of tectonic elements and surfaces. At the same time, this condensation creates an air of excitement and anticipation, a quality enhanced by the choice of materials, colour and lighting. The Cinémathèque québécoise is a further example of unexpected interpretations emerging from building in historical contexts and can rightly be seen in the lineage of such luminary precedents as the Town Hall Extension in Gothenburg.

While the Pavillon de design of the Université du Québec à Montréal completes an urban block, the resultant distinction in the open spaces around it – the open garden of the Habitations Jeanne-Mance to the north, the new square to the east and the alley to the south – gives the two principal facades of the Pavillon an exposed presence. Participating in these open spaces, the upper skylit gallery opens to the alley in the south via the cafeteria on the second floor and to the east through a continuous glazed slot overlooking the new square.

The spatial organization of the main circulation elements takes advantage of the narrow central slot, placing a promenading stairway from east to west, culminating in a roof terrace next to the library. Within this diversity of hallways, galleries and stairflights, visual and communicative interactions are possible. The choice of materials and construction elements supports the impression of diversity on the inside, though the similarity in the air conditioning ducts and the column cladding could be confusing. On the exterior, the Pavillon de design plays with a scalar jump: the two principal street facades stand in a relation of almost one to two, thereby once again underscoring the different external expectations. Here the detailing is more homogeneous and conventional, instituting an air of self-respect and dignity that gives the interior freedom. The Pavillon de design is a decent piece of architecture, making much, but not all, of the given opportunities that exist

Centre sportif de la Petite-Bourgogne

despite the challenges and constraints of site, program and cost. As such, the Medal for Merit for it is appropriate.

The Morris & Helen Belkin Art Gallery at the University of British Columbia is a convincing piece of architecture that develops from its context, sited in such a way as to complement the surrounding university fine arts facilities as well as the honorific Main Mall by locating the main entrance towards the outside visitor, while offering a minor entrance towards the teaching oriented eastern precinct. The building's three parts are clearly expressed in the configurational composition, each major junction underlined by figured roofs, walls, or rainwater spouts. The role of teaching finds an external assertion through the dominant linearity of the curved Mansard roof, which alludes to the bohemian atmosphere of Parisian roof garrets. The exhibition hall itself is quietly flexible, and simply lit.

Emerging from its section, the northern and southern ends of the Gallery are transfigured into something more than a section cut by the angular massing of the archives and print gallery, as well as the workshop and roof deck respectively. An indebtedness to the grand masters of abstract figuration, such as Picasso, can be understood in these compositions. At the Belkin Gallery, such allusions, as have been suggested here, are treated with recessive caution. Altogether, it represents a quiet celebration of architecture, giving the right doses of excitement or neutrality to the respective formal gestures and spaces; the Medal for Excellence is fully deserved.

The Centre sportif de la Petite-Bourgogne, located in a residential neighbourhood of Montreal, complete with a dominant church, massive school, external spaces and pedestrian routes through the blocks, takes part in the streetscape by massing the two major activities in two parallelepipeds around a top lit passage. In this way, the main street, rue Nôtre-Dame, is squarely addressed, giving views into and out of the Centre sportif. In containing the different programmatic parts so rigorously within the two distinctly coloured boxes (anthracite blocks for the pool and terracotta blocks for the gymnasium), subsequent orientation for the users becomes very clear. The colour coding is echoed on the interior walls (now blue tiles for the pool). The changing rooms for each of these facilities are located at the opposite ends so that the corridor is more equally loaded. The resultant location of the tall halls adds to the building's otherwise sparse configuration.

A perspectival game in the shaping of the windows to the pool adds a little spatial spice to an otherwise straightforward resolution of what in the eyes of the public and bureaucracy has become a rather mundane facility. Comparing the two parks in Toronto with this internal sports centre, the strife for autonomy from climatic vicissitudes, as expressed and enabled through architecture, becomes clear. While generally there is a larger degree of formal freedom in the case of exterior swimming pools, the task of sports centres has become so standardized that normative conditions have reduced the scope for architectural expression. Structural systems and materials are thus expected not only to appear to be efficient, but to be of such a basic type that the resultant building is in essence no more than an efficient box around the activities therein contained.

Having said all this, the Centre sportif de la Petite-Bourgogne should not be belittled for these reasons; nevertheless, an external observer should be forgiven for questioning the appropriateness of the Medal for Excellence in comparison with the other buildings in this category.

With reference to the above processes of autonomization from climatic conditions coupled with the debilitating entrenchment into normative expectations, the final two buildings with Medals for Merit can be understood to stand for the modest development in greater efficiencies in the use of resources, while at the same time not being free from the fundamental contradictions of building new fabric at the dual cost of neglecting existing structures on the one hand and the underprovision of finances to assure durability in construction for the newly built object. The Revenue Canada Building in Surrey, British Columbia, brings innovations such as individual work station centred environmental control and fair faced ceilings. Many of the other elements are worthy, such as the generally lower energy consumption and the greater use of daylight. However, the configuration and the detailing of the Revenue Canada Building, though carefully considered and realized, are, by comparison to other award buildings, unexceptional. Without doubt, the question of resource management and the ecological challenge to architecture are actually addressed by this building, but the answers it gives are modest. How many resources (financial, human capital and material) would have been saved by the reuse of an existing downtown building of the early twentieth century, with its mass construction, openable windows and easy access to public transport (thereby reducing individual car journeys)? Such an alternative solution, an equivalent to Strachan House, might also have gained a medal.

The National Archives of Canada in Gatineau, Québec, is the object of autonomization from all vicissitudes of life and climate per se. It stands in the trajectory of the orangeries of the Renaissance, the greenhouses of early industrialization and the vast domes by Buckminster Fuller. Here the aim is to sterilize the interior from all contamination from the outside, so as to eternalize the contents. The term Thermal Neutral Environment perfectly describes the technocratic approach to the task of preserving the national archive. In a mixture of temple structure and space age styling, the curved roof symbolizes the protective skin over the precious goods aided by the Heath-Robinsonesque, so-called piano

National Archives of Canada

stool-like columns, which are sometimes placed within the perimeter of the interior, sometimes without.

Given the unlimited distance that contemporary civilization has travelled from nature, the purpose of a national archive can be understood as today's equivalent to the tombs of the ancients: highly wrought with meaning, and yet struggling to find an appropriate form. Rather than seek parallels from nature, man has invented his own world of symbols and structures that are deemed to assure his continued existence. At the same time, notions of transience, of decay, passage and death are suppressed. All glistens in silver, refractive glass and high-tech exuberance. A failure in the air conditioning system, a major damage to the glazing system – where are the simple fail-safe devices? The National Archives of Canada is thus a metaphor for the curious state of our civilization: desiring to be free from all that constrains us, yet so vulnerable. The greater the apparent autonomy and the more advanced the level of comfort, the greater the height from which man can fall and the more disastrous the effect on the suppressed other.

The site of the National Archives is on the periphery of a suburb of Ottawa, Canada's capital. Ottawa is, like the majority of Canadian cities, at the southern edge of the vast territory. In this constant proximity to the dominant culture in the south and the flight from the inhospitable climate and the struggle to create a habitable environment, architecture in Canada is literally and conceptually on the edge. In this sense, the buildings awarded Medals for Excellence or Merit are paradigms for contemporary architecture across the globe: some for their architectural quality, some for the questions that they raise in the minds of external observers, as discussed above. From parks to the reuse of existing fabric, from urban interventions to greenfield offices or archives, there is a gamut of fundamentally different approaches to culture, to architecture, but above all to the way we, as a deeply disoriented global society, are willing to confront the increasingly ineluctable vicissitudes of the environment. There are buildings in Canada that are leading this search for a new direction, and as such, they too are on the edge.

© Wilfried Wang, November 1999

Être à la fine pointe:
À propos des Médailles du gouverneur général pour l'architecture de 1999

Wilfried Wang

Dans une civilisation mondiale encore dominée par la culture anglo-saxonne et la compt-abilité à court terme, les mises en garde des sociétés jouxtant cette culture dominante n'ont rien de surprenant; elles se fondent sur le principe que les cultures périphériques devraient se forger une identité propre afin de résister à l'hégémonie culturelle. Ces mises en garde soulèvent une série de questions sur la nature de cette identité; sa manifestation physique et sa composition; son lien avec le contexte matériel, la tradition et les effets permanents de l'aliénation sociale moderne et de l'abstraction culturelle. Toutes ces questions, si on y répond sérieusement, réfuteront indubitablement le principe posé. Et ces mises en garde, si on les analyse, révéleront l'origine de ces préoccupations. On les formule non pas tant par crainte de devenir une autre sous-culture de la culture dominante – quoiqu'il s'agisse d'un moment évident de résistance peu souvent justifié – que pour respecter la tradition d'actualiser, voire de façonner, un point de ralliement du peuple face à l'évolution galopante de tous les paramètres de la culture dominée.

Les sociétés du Nord, comme le Canada et la Scandinavie, se trouvent à la périphérie de la culture dominante du vingtième siècle, en l'occurrence celle des États-Unis. Pendant les deux siècles précédents, les cultures méditerranéennes de la France, de l'Italie et de la Grèce étaient le point de mire. Prises entre l'univers culturel légitimé par l'histoire et la géographie de l'Ancienne Europe et l'osmose culturelle irrésistible de l'idéal américain, les sociétés nordiques du début du siècle ont courtisé la pensée Richardsonienne. Tant l'architecture officielle d'Ottawa, que l'hôtel de ville et les édifices gouvernementaux de Stockholm ainsi que la gare d'Helsinki témoignent de cette idylle. Avant de pouvoir affirmer son identité particulière, cette architecture a dû vaincre le temps. Ces sociétés, en érigeant leurs monuments nationaux, ont transposé chez elles les pierres de Venise, adapté les éléments et les matériaux fragiles du climat doux du Sud à celui, rigoureux, du Nord, pour ralentir la dégradation inéluctable qu'entraîne le passage du temps. Les monuments nationaux romantiques du début du siècle sont maintenant des bastions isolés. Éparpillés sur un vaste territoire comme le Canada, ils témoignent tout juste d'une manœuvre péripatétique visant à stabiliser une jeune contrée. Cependant, cette soif actuelle d'identité, du moins comme elle s'exprime dans les discours des élus, ne se limite pas à ces bastions individuels mais vaut pour l'environnement collectif et représente par conséquent le rêve d'avoir un paysage culturel homogène, idéalisé dans les villages à flanc de colline, par exemple.

Ce rêve d'homogénéité superficielle est peut-être un moyen naïf de faire taire la crainte de devenir une sous-culture de la culture dominante. Sur toute la planète, bien que l'on puisse tracer des parallèles structuraux sous-jacents dans le façonnement d'une culture donnée – prenons par exemple l'automobile comme élément unifiant important avec les

contraintes qu'il impose à diverses infrastructures –, d'autres systèmes d'ordonnance-
ment qui ont transcendé le temps – tels les modèles de propriété qui donnent naissance
aux rythmes urbains – peuvent être une force dans l'apparence distincte d'un tissu social.
Toronto, Vancouver et Montréal sont peut-être influencées par l'architecture et l'urban-
isme américains mais elles présentent quand même des distinctions architecturales historiques. Certes, avec le temps, la fusion de terrains, la construction d'autoroutes ou la
fermeture de rues – sous l'effet des pressions de la mondialisation – peuvent signifier la
disparition de ces rythmes. Toutefois, à ce jour, ces distinctions sont encore visibles.

Dans un autre ordre d'idées, il faut se rappeler que les conditions topographiques et
le climat ont influencé le choix des constructions dans le passé. Les sociétés moins
favorisées ont dû apprendre à composer avec les forces de la nature. Elles ont dû choisir
leur emplacement, les matériaux et autres détails en fonction du vent et de la pluie, jauger
les distances à parcourir et les compétences artisanales à acquérir. De nos jours, les constructions et les instruments fabriqués par l'homme ont permis en grande partie de vaincre les vicissitudes de la nature. Seuls les grands désastres, comme les tempêtes ou les
tremblements de terre, mettent encore à l'épreuve la principale ligne de défense de l'être
humain : l'environnement bâti. Dans l'ensemble, cependant, les éléments du confort
comme l'éclairage artificiel, le chauffage et la ventilation, les constructions légères ou
robustes, les moyens de transport mécaniques, les capteurs solaires actifs et passifs, etc.,
ont permis à l'être humain de s'installer dans les régions les plus inhospitalières du
monde. Souvent, la nature est vue comme une source d'inspiration, ou plus généralement,
un cadre bucolique où ériger une architecture tout aussi sereine. Ou encore, elle est considérée comme un ensemble équilibré dans lequel l'architecture devrait s'intégrer. Ces
trois attitudes témoignent clairement de la relation romantique qui existe avec une nature
bienveillante, un système écologique qui, parce que l'être humain croit l'avoir maîtrisé et
juge donc qu'il ne menace plus son existence, offre plutôt une enveloppe maternelle qui
rétablit l'ordre des choses d'un geste protecteur et lui inspire des pensées poétiques.

Par contre, si le tissu bâti des siècles passés offre encore quelques « moments » de dif-
férence culturelle et que, par ailleurs, les méthodes de construction, les systèmes et les
mécanismes d'exploitation des édifices ont été conçus dans le but d'augmenter sans
cesse le confort, alors l'écart qui nous sépare de la nature vraie s'élargit tout autant. La
nature vraie, avec ses phénomènes catastrophiques occasionnels, encore imprévisibles,
auxquels se greffent l'influence catastrophique, graduelle et prévisible que l'être humain
a sur elle, est réprimée en tant que réalité. Les tremblements de terre ont entraîné la révi-
sion des normes de construction dans les zones menacées. Cependant, la consommation
illimitée des ressources avec ses conséquences graduelles et catastrophiques n'a pas

amené l'être humain à ralentir le processus de construction ni à en modifier sensiblement les méthodes. La nature vraie est indivisible, elle peut asséner des coups mortels et demeure, à ce jour, encore incontrôlable. Ce constat, même à ce stade avancé de la civilisation contemporaine, pourrait inciter les clients et les architectes à contenir leurs désirs d'ériger des monuments à leur propre vanité, et mettre ainsi un frein à la consommation d'ordre physique et esthétique. De plus, en ce qui concerne le caractère général d'une architecture respectueuse de la nature vraie, ce même constat pourrait faire s'exprimer avec une modestie palpable la force physique sublime et inspirante de la nature ainsi comprise, en mettant au jour la dépendance de l'être humain vis-à-vis d'elle.

L'architecture est donc l'indice de la distance par rapport à la nature vraie. Elle caractérise l'attitude de la civilisation à l'égard de la dépendance : la dépendance de l'environnement sous tous ses aspects, qu'il s'agisse du climat, de la société ou du tissu bâti. Traditionnellement, l'architecture a symbolisé la résistance aux forces de la nature, en les faisant comprendre par son existence même. En ce sens, l'architecture est le miroir de la nature, même si elle existe au sein d'elle. La notion de complémentarité de la nature pourrait permettre de définir une tout autre attitude. Ce sujet englobe un éventail de relations. Sous cet angle, l'architecture peut être considérée comme le prolongement fragile de l'enveloppe dont l'être humain a le plus directement besoin. Une telle enveloppe ne constituerait par conséquent qu'un simple intermédiaire, une prothèse entre les besoins de l'être humain et ceux de la nature, peut-être même les vicissitudes de la société. Dans son état final, l'architecture ainsi comprise révélerait sa fragilité et sa temporalité sous forme de ruines. En ce sens, l'architecture est loin d'affirmer la perfection, la pureté et la complétude; elle embrasse plutôt l'inadéquation humaine, en s'efforçant toujours de faire preuve d'ingéniosité afin de surmonter temporairement cette faiblesse.

Consciente de la finalité des ressources, l'architecture complémentaire établirait au minimum un équilibre fragile entre la constance de la nature et la fugacité de la présence humaine. Dans cette perspective, il est évident que la civilisation de la culture dominante anglo-saxonne ne fait que décorer la vraie nature, une civilisation dont le décor lui-même se dévoile graduellement. L'architecture de la culture dominante anglo-saxonne a un visage tellement barbare. L'architecture complémentaire prend plutôt en compte le caractère unique du lieu et du temps présents. Ce pourrait être une définition de l'identité.

En plaçant les médailles du Gouverneur général de 1999 dans ce contexte, deux éléments des parcs Ledbury et Rotary de Toronto composent directement avec le climat. Il n'est pas surprenant que le client, le ministères des Parcs et des Loisirs, ait donné la préférence à l'entretien facile et durable et se soit préoccupé des retombées environnementales de ces constructions. Les deux interventions proposent une piscine publique, le parc Ledbury offrant en plus une pataugeoire ou une patinoire. Dans leur contexte urbain, les deux études reprennent la forme orthogonale des environs, plaçant chaque configuration en forme de L sur son site respectif de sorte que des espaces ouverts et intelligibles soient délimités ou implicites. À la piscine du parc Rotary, on va même jusqu'à préserver un bouquet de saules et d'ormes sur la bordure sud.

Dans la composition architecturale des deux ensembles, on constate des différences significatives, notamment dans le traitement d'éléments relativement mineurs comme les voûtes de verdure ou les pergolas qui montrent la mission de l'édifice et son rapport avec le milieu — on y décèle un aménagement paysager, un construit artificiel ou naturel. Dans le cas de la piscine du parc Rotary, les éléments de la pergola partent, pour ainsi dire, d'une poutre cylindrique verticale soutenant une section en acier décentrée effilée en I, à laquelle sont fixées des poutrelles. On voit ici une forme parallèle à un tronc d'arbre, mais aussi l'ordre tectonique traditionnel des structures primaires et secondaires. Cette pergola est plus proche de la logique architecturale, c'est-à-dire de la logique formelle des structures formées de poutres, que celle du parc Ledbury. Dans ce dernier cas, le support vertical consiste en une grappe d'angles égaux qui s'étendent au-delà du plan inférieur des poutrelles du treillis de sorte que l'assemblage tectonique n'est pas immédiatement visible. Tous les éléments accessoires sont suspendus à la poutrelle principale. La composition fait plutôt penser à une structure végétale qu'à un ensemble de poutres. La légèreté de la pergola du parc Ledbury ne se répète pas dans la finition du toit de verdure qui aboutit au pavillon panoramique. Ici, un plan de panneaux de bois crée une surface fermée qui se démarque du décor végétal de la pergola.

Face aux deux catégories de médailles, soit la Médaille d'excellence et la Médaille du mérite, ces différences dans la finition des structures des deux parcs peuvent montrer les considérations qualitatives qui justifient ces distinctions. Le parc Ledbury, avec les diverses contradictions que l'on peut discerner dans l'exposition formelle des parties, est un essai de création d'un aménagement dur et artificiel, ou, en d'autres termes, une architecture dite d'aménagement. Avec son pont subtil, un croisement entre un Litzka et une structure de poutres laminées-collées — un élément quelque peu extravagant dans la composition globale (qu'est-ce qui n'est pas extravagant dans la bonne architecture, et pourtant si nécessaire à sa constitution ?) — le parc Ledbury est une exploration formelle dans un domaine différent et moins essayé du design architectural.

Sur un plan plus immédiat, l'ancienne mine Bruneau, qui abrite aujourd'hui le Centre d'intérêt minier de Chibougamau, confronte le visiteur au passé du site. Les murs de l'entrée et de l'intérieur de la galerie sont simplement recouverts de cuivre; rappel discret de l'exploitation. De même, la voie ferrée, comblée avec des planches de pin, constitue un

Rotary Park Pool

Cinémathèque québécoise

puissant élément de continuité, la mince ligne rouge en quelque sorte. La clôture grillagée de la soffite laisse subsister la menace d'un effondrement. L'ajout de meubles, le porte-manteaux, le comptoir d'accueil en cuivre ondulé, le lavabo en cuivre, et même le poste d'entrée mettent l'ancienne mine en vedette. Même si le mur recouvert de cuivre constitue un élément important d'orientation, avec son éclairage encastré à l'extrémité supérieure, et sa construction en panneaux qui révèle la substance au-delà de chacun, il est moins direct du point de vue construction que les autres éléments. De même, l'esprit du travail de l'architecte est digne d'éloges car il met en équilibre le nouvel usage et la première incursion humaine dans la nature.

La maison Strachan et la Cinémathèque québécoise sont deux autres reprises d'ouvrages existants. L'une des plus importantes entreprises de l'architecture contemporaine est sans aucun doute la préservation du tissu actuel mais adapté, si on considère que l'environnement bâti et l'industrie du bâtiment jouent un rôle central dans la gestion des ressources (énergie, émissions de carbone, etc.). En combinant ce principe à l'hébergement des sans-abri chroniques et, par surcroît, à leur participation active à la planification et à la construction de leurs futurs logis, on ne saurait s'attendre à une architecture de grande qualité. La remarquable conversion d'un entrepôt du dix-neuvième siècle à l'entrée du centre-ville de Toronto mérite d'autant plus de respect.

Le projet, étalé sur huit ans, a consisté à aménager une série marquante de chambres à coucher, de coins-repos et d'installations communautaires de manière à créer un intérieur urbain délimité clairement par des espaces de transition que l'on pourrait décrire comme des « rues » et des lieux de rassemblement devant l'entrée des logements, et que les architectes appellent l'agora ou le porche. Les sans-abri sont attirés par la rue parce qu'elle offre de nombreuses portes de sortie. La liberté de mouvement et la visibilité nette le long des passages courbes à l'intérieur de la maison Strachan étaient donc d'une importance suprême. Il fallait en outre éviter les corridors droits qui auraient donné à l'édifice des allures d'institution. Les courbures des passages identifient bien chaque logis. Des porches et des pergolas marquent les seuils de chaque étage aussi haut qu'un loft.

À ce titre, il se dégage de la construction, pour laquelle on a utilisé du bois rude, du contreplaqué et d'autres matériaux en feuilles au fini lisse, l'impression d'une « rue » intérieure, d'où il doit être possible de s'échapper et, en même temps, le sentiment essentiel de pouvoir se réfugier dans sa cellule. La disposition des couloirs, des salons et de la place de « l'hôtel de ville » est ingénieuse : elle permet des formes multiples d'occupation, pour lesquelles on a d'ailleurs fait appel à des artistes et à des artisans. La maison Strachan est la synthèse exemplaire d'un besoin fondamental, réalisée dans une architecture tout à fait appropriée, une architecture qui fait passer ses usagers au premier plan et célèbre l'esprit de l'ouvrage dans les moindres détails.

Pour sa part, la Cinémathèque québécoise, à Montréal, réunit deux édifices dont le trait d'union est l'entrée à laquelle se greffent une salle de cinéma supplémentaire, une salle de vidéo et une cafétéria. Au lieu de combler l'espace vide entre les structures de maçonnerie existantes, le nouvel édifice prévoit un espace extérieur qui vient éclairer les zones de circulation, et qui dessine une cour menant à la cafétéria. L'entrée principale, un hall généreux qui sert d'espace de projection et permet aux visiteurs de s'orienter facilement, est donc située là où se trouve maintenant le nouveau centre du complexe. Les éléments sont disposés en couches, presque épisodiques et à multiples facettes, de sorte que l'on n'a jamais l'impression d'être dans un lieu où tout est calculé.

L'intégration de l'ancien et du nouveau, à l'intérieur et à l'extérieur, s'affirme brillamment en avant de la vieille école : ici, la passerelle en acier de l'étage supérieur de l'entrée forme un écran d'un côté et, de l'autre, soutient un écran de projection. Le nouveau plan met à l'avant l'école, normalement légèrement en retrait, alignant ainsi les deux édifices sur une ligne graduellement fuyante. L'entremêlement de l'image et des usagers, l'autre idée centrale derrière le concept architectural, devient la projection eidétique dans le domaine public. L'ancien et le nouveau sont juxtaposés dans une condensation superposée d'éléments et de surfaces tectoniques. De même, cette concentration suscite l'animation et l'anticipation, une atmosphère encore rehaussée par le choix des matériaux, de la couleur et de l'éclairage. La Cinémathèque québécoise est un autre exemple des interprétations inattendues des constructions situées dans des emplacements historiques et peut, à juste titre, s'inscrire dans la lignée de précédents géniaux comme l'agrandissement de l'hôtel de ville de Göteborg.

En complétant un bloc urbain, le Pavillon de design de l'Université du Québec à Montréal crée, entre les espaces ouverts qui l'entourent – le jardin des Habitations Jeanne-Mance au nord, la nouvelle place à l'est et la ruelle au sud –, une distinction qui met en relief les deux façades principales du pavillon. Participant à ces espaces ouverts, la galerie supérieure éclairée par un puits de lumière s'ouvre au sud sur la ruelle en traversant la cafétéria au deuxième étage, et à l'est en devenant une faille vitrée qui surplombe la nouvelle place.

L'organisation spatiale des principaux éléments de circulation exploite la faille étroite du centre, qu'un escalier sillonne d'est en ouest, et qui se termine sur la toiture-terrasse près de la bibliothèque. Dans cette diversité de couloirs, de galeries et d'escaliers, les interactions visuelles et les communications sont possibles. Le choix des matériaux et des éléments de construction renforce cette impression de diversité à l'intérieur, quoique les conduits de climatisation et le revêtement des colonnes se ressemblent étrangement. À l'extérieur, le Pavillon de design joue sur deux plans : les deux façades principales sont en rapport de simple au double, faisant encore plus ressortir les différentes attentes externes. Ici, les détails sont homogènes et conventionnels, ils commandent un sentiment de respect de soi et de dignité qui donne la liberté intérieure. Le Pavillon de design est un ouvrage décent qui exploite une bonne part de possibilités malgré les défis et les contraintes de l'emplacement, du programme et des coûts. À ce titre, la Médaille du mérite qui lui a été attribuée est légitime.

La Morris & Helen Belkin Art Gallery de l'University of British Columbia est une pièce convaincante d'architecture qui se marie avec l'environnement car elle est implantée de manière à apporter un complément à l'édifice des beaux-arts et au Main Mall honorifique. En effet, l'entrée principale accueille d'abord le visiteur qui vient de l'extérieur tandis qu'une entrée secondaire permet d'accéder au bâtiment de l'est dédié à l'enseignement. Les trois parties de l'édifice se détachent clairement dans la configuration de l'ensemble, chaque carrefour principal étant souligné par l'ornementation des toits, des murs ou des conduites pluviales. La mission d'enseignement s'affirme à l'extérieur dans la linéarité dominante de la toiture à la mansarde, qui rappelle l'atmosphère bohème des combles parisiens. La salle d'exposition est facilement adaptable et éclairée simplement.

Surgissant de leur section, les extrémités nord et sud de la galerie se transforment en quelque chose qui est plus qu'une section coupée par la masse angulaire des archives et

Pavillon de design de l'Université du Québec à Montréal

The Morris and Helen Belkin Art Gallery

de la galerie des estampes, ainsi que par l'atelier et la toiture-terrasse. On dénote dans ses compositions une dette envers les grands maîtres de l'art figuratif abstrait, tel Picasso. À la galerie Belkin, ces allusions sont traitées avec une prudence extrême. Dans l'ensemble, l'ouvrage est un hommage discret à l'architecture où la stimulation et la neutralité s'équilibrent dans les gestes et les espaces formels. La Médaille d'excellence est pleinement méritée.

Le Centre sportif de la Petite-Bourgogne est situé dans un quartier résidentiel de Montréal, doté d'une église imposante et d'une école massive, de pâtés de maisons jalonnés de voies piétonnières. Il s'intègre dans le paysage des rues en rassemblant les deux principales activités dans deux parallélépipèdes qui bordent un passage éclairé par le dessus. Ainsi construite, la rue principale, la rue Notre-Dame, offre une vue à l'intérieur et à l'extérieur du Centre sportif. En groupant les différents programmes d'activités aussi rigoureusement dans les deux blocs de couleurs distinctes (anthracite pour la piscine et terracota pour le gymnase), les visiteurs s'orientent aisément. Le code des couleurs se répète sur les murs intérieurs (de la céramique bleue pour la piscine). Les vestiaires de chaque unité sont situés aux extrémités du corridor afin de répartir la circulation. De par leur emplacement, les hautes salles meublent la configuration de l'édifice qui serait autrement clairsemée.

Le jeu de perspectives des fenêtres qui donnent sur la piscine ajoute un peu de piquant à une résolution par ailleurs simple devenue, aux yeux du public et de la bureaucratie, une installation plutôt banale. La comparaison des deux parcs de Toronto avec ce centre de sports intérieurs révèle la lutte qu'il faut mener pour s'affranchir des aléas climatiques. Bien que l'on dénote en général, une plus grande liberté formelle dans le traitement des piscines extérieures, la tâche des centres sportifs est devenue tellement standardisée que les exigences normatives ont réduit la marge d'expression architecturale. Les systèmes et les matériaux structuraux doivent non seulement paraître efficaces mais aussi être tellement élémentaires que l'édifice qui en résulte n'est essentiellement pas davantage qu'une boîte fonctionnelle abritant les activités qui s'y déroulent.

Ceci dit, on ne saurait déprécier le Centre sportif de la Petite-Bourgogne pour ces raisons, mais il faudrait pardonner l'observateur qui s'interroge sur le bien-fondé de la décision d'attribuer la Médaille d'excellence à cet édifice en particulier par rapport aux autres édifices de cette catégorie.

En ce qui concerne les moyens utilisés pour vaincre les conditions climatiques et l'intégration débilitante d'attentes normatives, on peut voir dans les deux derniers édifices qui ont reçu la Médaille du mérite, des témoins de l'utilisation plus efficace des ressources. Parallèlement, toutefois, ils illustrent l'assujettissement aux contradictions fondamentales de la construction d'un nouveau tissu dont le prix est double : négliger les structures existantes et se passer des fonds nécessaires pour assurer la durabilité du nouvel édifice. Le bâtiment de Revenu Canada à Surrey, en Colombie-Britannique, apporte des innovations : par exemple, le contrôle environnemental axé sur le poste de travail individuel, et les plafonds à parement clair. Nombre d'autres éléments sont dignes d'intérêt, notamment la consommation généralement faible d'énergie et la grande utilisation de la lumière du jour. Cependant, la configuration et la finition de l'édifice de Revenu Canada, bien qu'elles aient été soigneusement étudiées et réalisées, ne sont pas exceptionnelles par comparaison avec d'autres édifices primés. La conception de cet édifice apporte indubitablement une réponse au problème de la gestion des ressources et au défi écologique, mais elle est modeste. Combien de ressources (financières, humaines et matérielles) aurait-on pu économiser en réutilisant un édifice du centre-ville du début du vingtième siècle, avec sa construction massive, ses fenêtres qui s'ouvrent et un accès facile au transport en commun (ce qui aurait réduit par le fait même les trajets individuels en automobile)? Une solution de ce genre, à l'instar de celle que propose la maison Strachan, aurait pu également mériter une médaille.

Revenue Canada Building

L'édifice des Archives nationales du Canada, à Gatineau, au Québec, est la matérialisation même de l'isolement contre les vicissitudes de la vie et du climat. Il s'inscrit dans la lignée des orangeries de la Renaissance, des serres du début de l'ère industrielle et des vastes dômes créés par Buckminster Fuller. Ici, le but est de protéger l'intérieur de toute contamination externe afin d'assurer la pérennité de son contenu. L'expression « environnement thermique neutre » décrit parfaitement l'approche technocratique de la préservation des archives nationales. Alliant la structure d'un temple et le style de l'ère spatiale, le toit en voûte symbolise la membrane de protection qui recouvre des biens précieux et repose sur des colonnes à la Heath-Robinson, c'est-à-dire des colonnes rappelant un tabouret de piano, tantôt placées sur le périmètre intérieur, tantôt sur le périmètre extérieur.

Compte tenu de la distance illimitée que la civilisation contemporaine a mise entre elle et la nature, on peut comprendre que les archives nationales sont à la société d'aujourd'hui ce que les tombeaux étaient aux peuples de l'Antiquité : lourdement chargées de signification et, pourtant, luttant pour se trouver une forme appropriée. Plutôt que de chercher des parallèles avec la nature, l'être humain a inventé son propre monde de symboles et de structures qui sont censés assurer sa pérennité. Par ailleurs, les notions d'éphémère, de détérioration, de passage et de mort sont éliminées. Tout brille d'un éclat argenté, verre réfractaire et exubérance techno. Si le système de climatisation tombe en panne, si le vitrage est sérieusement endommagé, où sont les simples dispositifs de sécurité? Les Archives nationales sont donc une métaphore représentative de la curieuse situation de notre civilisation : désireuse de se libérer de tout ce qui la limite, et pourtant si vulnérable. Plus l'autonomie apparente est grande et plus le confort est avancé, plus longue sera la chute de l'homme et plus désastreux seront les effets.

Les Archives nationales sont situées à la périphérie de la banlieue d'Ottawa, la capitale du Canada, qui à l'instar de la majorité des villes du pays, est implantée au sud de ce vaste territoire. À cause de la présence constante de la culture dominante du Sud, de l'éloignement des climats inhospitaliers et du combat à mener pour créer un environnement habitable, l'architecture canadienne est littéralement et conceptuellement à la fine pointe. En ce sens, les édifices qui ont obtenu la Médaille d'excellence ou la Médaille du mérite sont des paradigmes de l'architecture contemporaine du monde entier : certains pour leur qualité architecturale, d'autres pour le questionnement qu'il suscite chez les observateurs de l'extérieur, comme on l'a vu plus haut. Des parcs aux édifices recyclés, en passant par les interventions urbaines, les bureaux ou les archives complètement nouveaux, il existe une pléthore d'approches fondamentalement différentes de la culture et de l'architecture, mais par-dessus tout, de façons dont nous, en tant que société globale profondément désorientée, sommes prêts à faire face aux vicissitudes de plus en plus inéluctables de l'environnement. Au Canada, il existe des édifices qui donnent le ton de cette recherche de nouvelles directions, et, en ce sens, ils sont aussi à la fine pointe.

© Wilfried Wang, novembre 1999

Medals for Excellence / Médailles d'excellence

The Morris and Helen Belkin Art Gallery

Strachan House

Centre d'intérêt minier de Chibougamau

Centre sportif de la Petite-Bourgogne

Ledbury Park

The Morris and Helen Belkin Art Gallery

Peter Cardew Architects

PROJECT DESCRIPTION: Located at the north end of the Main Mall at the University of British Columbia, the Belkin Gallery formally anchors this organizing boulevard and completes the Arts Precinct, a group of modernist buildings for the schools of music, architecture, fine arts and theatre. The form of the building acknowledges its role as marker with a tower at the prominent corner of the precinct.

Within the facility are three related gallery spaces, a separate print gallery, curatorial work spaces, administrative offices and a dedicated archive. Conceived as both educational facility and gallery, the building encourages the overlap and interaction of public and service spaces to cultivate a better appreciation of support functions in the operation of a gallery.

A single circulation spine serves the galleries and their support spaces, the exhibition and holding areas, and the curatorial workspace. These support functions are accessed through a series of rolling steel doors that forms a wall to the public hall and the galleries opposite, while the administrative offices overlook the public space from above.

Integral to this notion of pliant space is a flexible gallery arrangement, achieved through a pair of rotating walls that enable the galleries to be reconfigured to suit the needs of each exhibition. Canted glazing above the eastern wall of the three gallery spaces provides views of movement and change in the crowns of the oak trees lining the Main Mall. This presumes that the gallery experience is enhanced by allowing diversionary views to the outside, and questions current attitudes toward natural daylight.

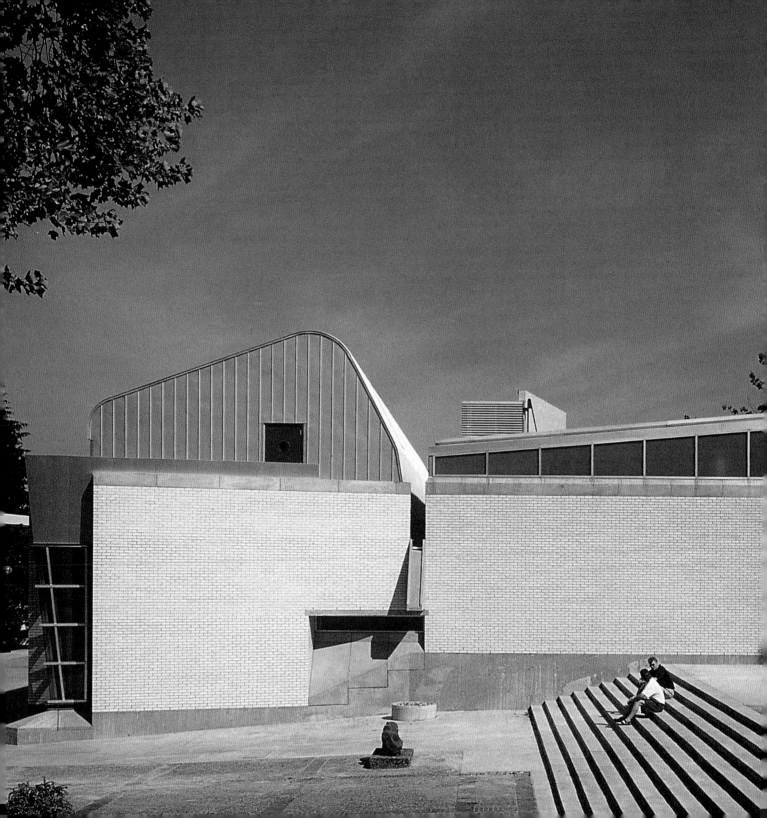

The exterior form of the gallery allows access from both the Arts Precinct plaza and the Main Mall, while developing the formal and informal qualities of each. This extends the ambiguity of the interior spaces to the exterior, where the plaza entry doubles as a loading dock and acts as a counterpoint to the constrained formality of the Mall entrance. To contrast the intrinsically introverted nature of the gallery building and its possible interpretation as an exclusive facility, the canopies at both entrances exhibit an amplified structural gesture as a hospitable focus, framed by large, unpenetrated wall surfaces.

The steel structure of the building is exposed on the interior as a skeletal framework supported on concrete bases and wrapped with glazed brick at the walls and with metal at the roof. The glazed brick is identical to that used on surrounding buildings dating from the late fifties and early sixties. The roof forms a valley that defines the gallery spaces on one side of the interior and the curatorial and administrative spaces on the other. Outside, the valley collects the rainwater, which is discharged through precast concrete scuppers at either end of the building.

The building is approximately 15,000 sq. ft., with a third of its area allocated to each of the principal components: exhibition space, curatorial functions and administration.

JURY COMMENT: "The Belkin Gallery on the campus of the University of British Columbia is a simple, clear volumetric composition, clad in beautiful white brick. The interior spaces are exhilarating and the building is rigorously detailed without becoming fetishized. Although there are some minor problems with controlling the large amounts of natural light, on the whole this is what I would call "deep architecture" because it feels fresh and new, while simultaneously taking a quiet place in the now long history of twentieth-century clean 'White Modernism.'" **Larry Richards**

PROJECT CREDITS
Building: The Morris and Helen Belkin Art Gallery
Architect: Peter Cardew Architects
Building address: University of British Columbia,
Vancouver, BC
Location: Main Mall, UBC campus
Client: University of British Columbia (Scott Watson,
Director, The Morris and Helen Belkin Art Gallery)
Architect team: Peter Cardew, Marc Boutin, Janne
Corniel, Don Kasko; Peter Wood (modelmaker)
Structural: C.Y. Loh Associates
Mechanical & electrical: D.W. Thompson
Landscape: Christopher Phillips & Associates
Lighting: Gabriel/Design
Museum consultant: Murray Frost
Contractor: Landmark Construction
Budget: $2.9 million
Photography: Timothy Hursley / Peter Cardew Architects

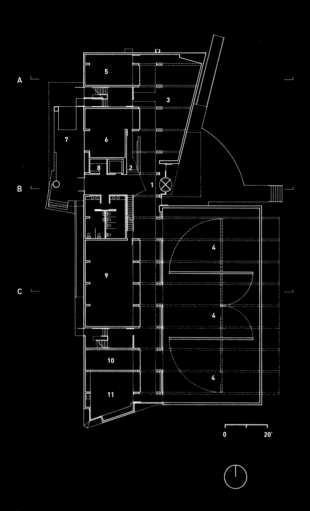

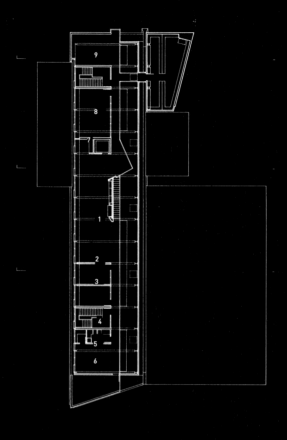

0   20'

42   **Ground floor plan**
1. Foyer 2. Reception 3. Print gallery 4. Gallery
5. Crate storage 6. Shipping and receiving
7. Loading dock 8. Coats 9. Permanent holding
10. Storage 11. Curatorial workshop

Second floor plan
1. General office 2. Director 3. Associate curator
4. Kitchen 5. Conference room 6. Deck
7. Copy room 8. Library/archivist 9. Seminar room
10. Archives

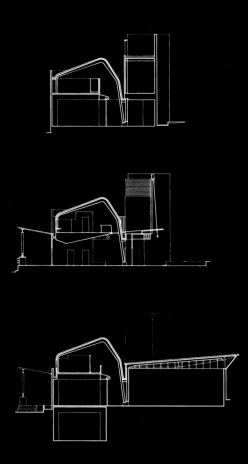

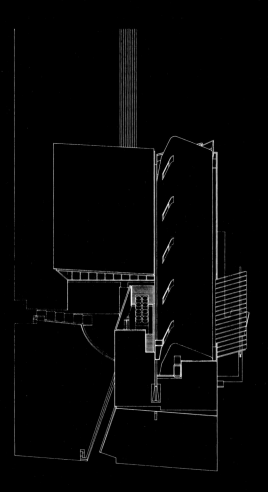

46   **Section A**
        Section B
        Section C

Axonometric

Strachan House

Levitt Goodman Architects Ltd.

PROJECT DESCRIPTION: Strachan House is an innovative housing prototype in a renovated, three-story 19th-century warehouse in Toronto. It opened in December 1996 to provide short- and long-term shelter to seventy chronically homeless men and women. Since then, Strachan House residents have formed an elaborate community that is largely self-governing.

The basic concept of the design, "the outside coming in," is expressed through spatial organization, materials and details. Most of Strachan House is given over to public and semi-public uses (unlike conventional apartment living, where private spaces are privileged). The building is organized in an urban way as a hierarchy of spaces from the private bedroom to the collective "house," to the neighbourhood "street," and finally to the Town Hall for the whole community. At the end of each horizontal street is a three-story atrium with a stairway that permits continuous movement through the various public rooms in the building. During bi-weekly meetings, the Town Hall atrium becomes part theatre, part observatory, as residents participate from various levels, perches and vantage points.

Transitional spaces in the building are clearly defined. Along the streets, the front porch of each house is defined by a suspended trellis made of rough cut timber and peeled wooden poles. Inside each house is another, more intimate set of front porches with smaller trellises clad in stained plywood panels that mark the transition between the collective house and each private bedroom.

"Savard's" is a house-within-a-house at the east end of the ground floor and was designed to house women for whom Toronto's emergency shelter system is inaccessible due to violent behaviour and/or extreme emotional behaviour. For various reasons, conventional bedrooms are anathema to this client group. For some, enclosed spaces with beds are characterized as "male"; for others, bedrooms are reminders of past trauma; for still others, bedrooms represent a former intimate life that is now long gone. Consequently, a "nook" was developed as an alternate model of domesticity: a semi-enclosed, modular unit with a curtain to control visual privacy. This architectural proposition bridges the extremes of experience defined by the fixed space of a bedroom and the nomadic existence of street life.

Various artists worked collaboratively with architects from the early stages of the project, so that art and architecture could proceed as integral elements of the design process. The exchange of ideas and expertise stretched each other's aesthetic assumptions and limitations, and resulted in an environment that is far richer than if the two disciplines had been kept separate. Eventual residents of the building were also involved throughout its design and construction, leading to a highly sensitive project that responds to the particular client group and the physical context.

JURY COMMENT: "Ce projet est tout à fait surprenant. Le recyclage du bâtiment industriel est ingénieux et très généreux. Situé un peu à l'écart, l'ensemble offre une intimité appréciable. Son relatif isolement de la ville est contrebalancé par une structure interne souple qui facilite les rapports entre les habitants. Et c'est sans doute là l'un des aspects les plus remarquables du projet qui est relativement simple et ouvert et dont les problèmes techniques, liés au code par exemple, donnent lieu à des solutions qui enrichissent le projet. Les relations verticale d'un étage à l'autre sont généreusement exploitée. Elles sont gérées par des dispositifs de fermeture qui loin d'être oppressifs contribuent à renforcer l'impression générale du bâtiment, celle d'un habitat vivant et chaleureux qui rappelle sous certains aspects l'architecture d'Aldo van Eyck." **Anne Cormier**

53

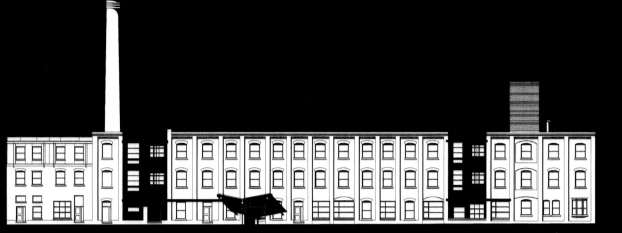

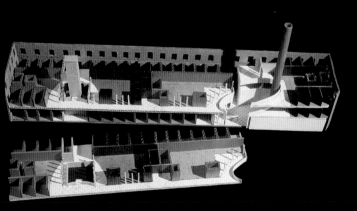

PROJECT CREDITS
Building: Strachan House
Architect: Levitt Goodman Architects Ltd.
Building address: 53 Strachan Avenue, Toronto, ON
Location: at Wellington Street, three blocks west of Bathurst Street
Client: Homes First Society
Architect team: Dean Goodman (partner-in-charge), Wyn Bielaska, Filiz Klassen, Greg Latimer, Marko Lavrisa, Stephen Leblanc, Janna Levitt, Richard Milgrom, David Stavros
Structural: Balke Engineering Inc.
Mechanical & electrical: Lam and Associates Ltd.
Restoration: E.R.A. Architects Inc.
Fire & life safety: Arencon Inc.
Environmental: Holocene Consultants
Artists: Scott Childs, Steven Marshall, David Warne, Paul Raff, Rae Bridgman, Robert Burley, Debra Friedman
Construction management: JAC-Andersen
Budget: $3.3 million
Photography: Robert Burley/Design Archive

Wellington Street elevation

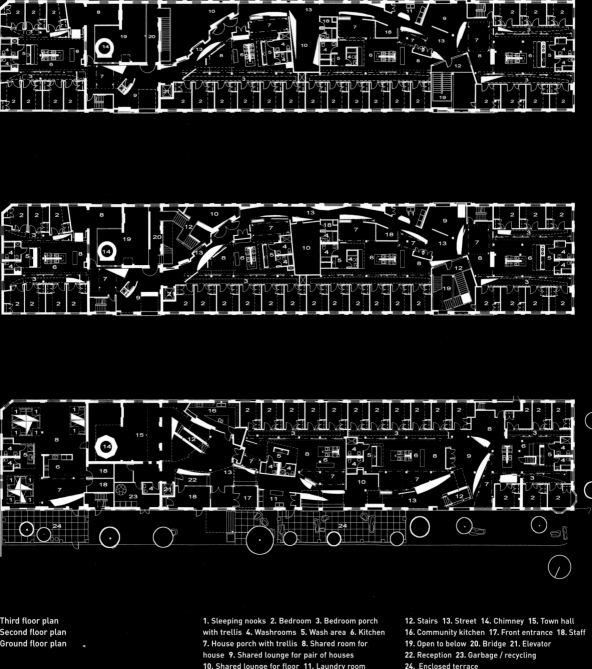

Third floor plan
Second floor plan
Ground floor plan

1. Sleeping nooks 2. Bedroom 3. Bedroom porch
with trellis 4. Washrooms 5. Wash area 6. Kitchen
7. House porch with trellis 8. Shared room for
house 9. Shared lounge for pair of houses
10. Shared lounge for floor 11. Laundry room

12. Stairs 13. Street 14. Chimney 15. Town hall
16. Community kitchen 17. Front entrance 18. Staff
19. Open to below 20. Bridge 21. Elevator
22. Reception 23. Garbage / recycling
24. Enclosed terrace

Centre d'intérêt minier de Chibougamau

Julien Architectes et Les architectes Plante et Julien

PROJECT DESCRIPTION: This project is embedded inside an abandoned copper mine near Chibougamau, Québec, about 700 kilometres north of Montréal. The mine had been discovered behind a huge mound of debris by a local explorer. The new interpretation centre, with its rock-hewn galleries and technical services, supports expeditions into the bowels of the mountain and the history of mining.

Concept: The sheer vastness of the stark landscape and the dramatic effect of a solitary opening in the face of the mountain prompted a decision to build the interpretation centre inside the mine rather than to build a new structure outside. The original mound of debris, supplemented by rock excavated from the mine, was reused to build entrance ramps outside. To suggest that this was once a copper mine where ore was eventually transformed into polished metal, a linear wall clad in natural copper now rises from the earth and extends from the entrance and exhibit galleries into the interior of the mine. Its 1.9–metre height is human-scale and emphasizes the confines of the interior tunnels and spaces.

    The copper wall is the only visible exterior element: a marker for hidden treasures and dangers beyond. It also serves as a utility wall for lighting, mechanical and electrical components throughout the interpretation centre. Lighting units inserted into the top of the wall create a general glow that illuminates the rock ceiling, in contrast to the stronger lighting used for the lateral exhibit spaces.

Materials: With a modest budget, the materials had to be carefully selected and additional excavation had to be strategic. The new spaces and vaults were created by surgical excavation and blasting, with surprising precision and efficiency.

The materials used are generally found in mines: rock and galvanized steel, with rough spruce planks for cupboards, partitions and doors. Floors in the exhibit areas are covered in fine crushed gravel, and the rock ceiling is covered in wire safety mesh. The materials are allowed to age naturally in the underground and exterior environments, and will slowly acquire an oxidized patina.

Since water is ever-present inside the mine, the equipment, furniture, finishes and accessories were designed to resist the ravages of moisture. Suspended copper domes and awnings also protect staff and sensitive equipment.

Exhibits: Visitors arrive at a reception desk resembling a huge copper spool, then proceed into the permanent exhibit area that is located in three vaulted rooms that have been excavated from the rock. In the cloakroom they don overcoats, boots and helmets. Beyond a heavy door the visitors can then explore more than two kilometres of shafts and galleries, illuminated only by the headlights on their helmets. Sound and light installations further reveal the treasures of this dark underground universe.

JURY COMMENT: "A lack of means is translated into a simple, clear and strong idea. The project is as straightforward as lighting a tunnel and letting people go in to see what it looks like. In this way, it minimizes interference and allows exploration. Interpretation is the experience of exploration. The project's weakest points in fact appear to be the points of greatest interference." **Stephen Teeple**

PROJECT CREDITS
Building: Centre d'intérêt minier de Chibougamau
Architect: Julien Architectes et Les architectes
Plante et Julien
Building address: Chibougamau, Québec
Location: 700 kilometres north of Montréal,
12 kilometres northeast of Chibougamau
Client: Municipalité de Chibougamau
Architect team: Marc Julien (principal-in-charge),
Stéphane Carrière, Michael Boxer
Structural, mechanical & electrical: Gérin-Lajoie,
Experts Conseils Inc.
Mining engineering: Roche Ltée
Exhibit design: Idéation Communications
Contractor: Larouche Construction
Budget: $650,000
Photography: Jean-François Lenoir

Section through exhibit room

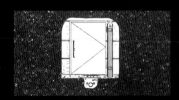

Section through tunnel

Plan / Section
1. Path **2.** Debris mound (mock) **3.** Entrance terrace   **10.** Permanent exhibit room **11.** Vertical shaft
4. Main gate **5.** Main gallery **6.** Washrooms   **12.** Existing rails **13.** Boots and helmet room
7. Mechanical room **8.** Reception desk **9.** Boutique   **14.** Gate to mining complex

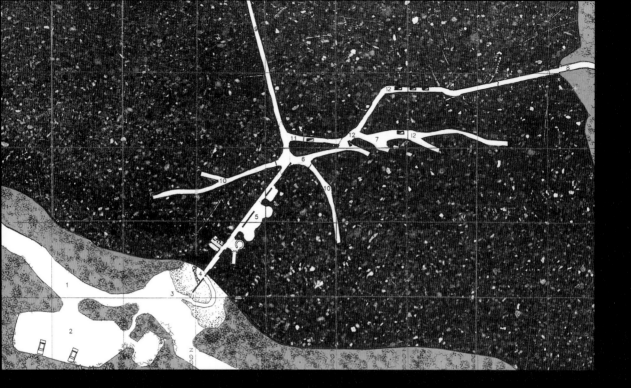

0   80'

Site plan

1. Access road 2. Parking 3. Debris mound /
entrance path 4. Mine entrance 5. New exhibit
gallery 6. Existing mining complex 7. Sound and
light display 8. Alternative exit

9. To other galleries 10. Condemned galleries
11. Mining display 12. Vertical shafts (animated
exhibits)

Centre sportif de la Petite-Bourgogne

Saia et Barbarese, architectes

PROJECT DESCRIPTION: In this southern part of Montreal the neighbourhood of Petite-Bourgogne adjoins various condominium and apartment complexes near rue Notre-Dame. Buildings here stand shoulder-to-shoulder with others that are older, of similar size, in brick and stone of various colours. Together, the buildings present an irregular appearance, but traditional order is maintained by the regular grid pattern of streets. This is where a local gathering place has now been created.

The new sports centre blends into its surroundings while also proclaiming its own presence. Its two powerful monoliths are in scale with the surrounding structures, and the colours and textures of the new building complement those of the existing buildings. However, its unusual size of brick, the use of mortar in the same colour, the play of openings, and the galvanized metal arise from a more contemporary vocabulary.

The first mass of red brick becomes a symbol of earth for the gymnasium while the second mass of anthracite brick becomes a symbol of water for the swimming pool. They face each other across a broad enclosed mall. This mall, paved in stone, follows the course of an old laneway and leads from a pedestrian walk along Petite-Bourgogne School all the way to rue Notre-Dame. An entrance opens at each of its ends. Inside, light floods through the skylights in a pattern that changes with every hour of the day. On the gymnasium side, the sunlight is filtered by cubes of blue-tinted glass and sheltering tongues of perforated metal. On the pool side, a stronger shade of blue colours an area of ceramic tile while a broad indent guides the eye up and out of the park, toward the city skyline. In the

evening, the regular openings in the dark walls shine like stars while continuing to serve as noise baffles.

The building design follows the simple organizational concept of two different but symmetrical spaces linked by an access area. The passerby instantly grasps the purpose of the building while the user of the sports centre grasps the purity and efficiency of its architecture.

JURY COMMENT: "This project succeeds in its robust and sometimes raw use of space, material and scale. Its relation to its site works well, using only a few limited devices at appropriate urban scale. Its interior circulation space gains its force through careful visual connection to the activities of the building and compelling moments of light that stretch space and draw the eye. This is not a building that relies on detail. It gains its effect by minimal means, robustly conceived. It invents with a tremendous economy of means." **Patricia Patkau**

Floor plan

1. Swimming pool 2. Wading pool 3. Access area
4. Gymnasium 5. Men's lockers 6. Women's lockers
7. Multipurpose room

8. Meeting room 9. Office 10. Day care
11. Restaurant 12. Storage 13. Family lockers

PROJECT CREDITS
Building: Centre sportif de la Petite-Bourgogne
Architect: Saia et Barbarese, architectes
Building address: 1825 rue Notre-Dame ouest,
Montréal, QC
Location: two blocks west of rue Guy
Client: Service des Immeubles/Ville de Montréal
Architect team: Mario Saia (project architect), Dino
Barbarese, Vladimir Topouzanov, David
Griffin, James Aitken
Structural: MLC Associés
Mechanical & electrical: Soprin/Sima
Landscape: Gunta Mackars Landscape Architecture
Contractor: Les constructions Lavacon Inc.
Budget: $7 million
Photography: Michel Brunelle

Ledbury Park

Shim-Sutcliffe Architects / G+G Partnership Architects

PROJECT DESCRIPTION: Ledbury Park began with the creation of a site. A new, artificially constructed topographic condition provides the context for this recreational facility and its surrounding landscape. The park's architectural and landscape features are integrated and interwoven throughout the project. Water weaves throughout the site, creating a physical link among various programmatic elements.

Context and surroundings: The site was a level, three-acre park that occupies the leftover portions of a residential suburban block just north of Toronto. The juxtaposition of modest post-war bungalows and newer maximum-envelope stucco boxes illustrated the need for a new community centre and a new neighbourhood focus. The Parks and Recreation Department was an enlightened client from the outset: they wanted to create a timeless project for the neighbourhood, while also addressing long-term maintenance and operational issues.

Programme: Ledbury Park includes a sunken 50 x 300-foot pleasure skating canal that transforms into a shallow reflecting pool during the warmer months. A circular outdoor wading pool and a 25 x 75-foot swimming pool are elevated three feet above grade to provide a vantage point for viewing the park. A 3,500-square-foot, linear brick change building serves the outdoor swimming pool and its adjacent year-round viewing pavilion serves the skating canal. A series of primary and secondary walkways, two pedestrian bridges

and a plaza connect the park to its surrounding neighbourhood. A large mechanical room occupies the lower level of the change building and contains both filtration and refrigeration equipment.

Rebuilding a new topographic condition: A new, artificial topography was constructed upon the existing terrain. The skating canal / reflecting pool is contained within an elongated rectangular plane set a few feet below grade; the excavated fill is used to form an earth berm, creating a grassy embankment. A cor-ten steel pedestrian bridge links both sides of the canal and provides elevated views of the rest of the park from the pool deck. A long brick building with a wooden trellis and boardwalk houses swimming pool changerooms and links the pool and the canal.

Integration of architecture and landscape: Brick garden walls and a dense row of pyramidal English oaks and custom-designed lamp standards line the main pedestrian route through the site. The elevated pedestrian walk that circumnavigates the skating canal / reflecting pool is defined on one side by a formal allée of pleached lindens, and on the other two sides by a picturesque walk between sumachs, oaks and maples. The role of water in winter and summer was carefully orchestrated to provide different qualities during each season. The architectural promenade weaves together the custom cor-ten steel pedestrian bridge, wooden boardwalks, viewing pavilions, groves and allées of trees, and an articulated public plaza. Integrating these simple elements into a public landscape offers a rich spatial experience for all visitors.

JURY COMMENT: "This project invents its own site in a compelling manner. By cut and fill, it identifies a site that didn't exist before the project intervened – a richer, more three-dimensional site. Its achievements lie in the multiplicity of site identities it manages to establish. Its architecture seems most compelling when aiding in establishing that richness of place: providing sequence, forming places tucked down in the land and paths above, using rows and grids of trees to occupy the modified topography, forming edges above, overlooks to and filtered views through." **Patricia Patkau**

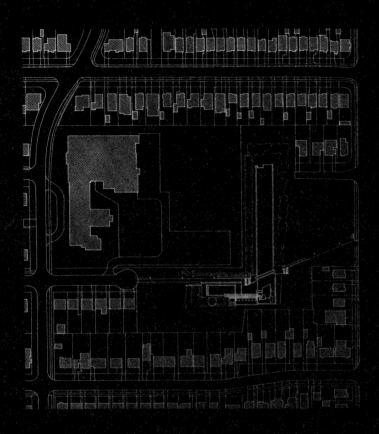

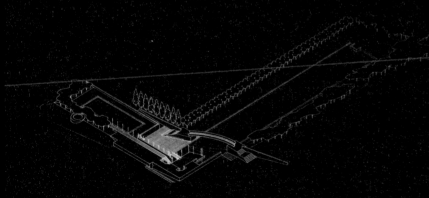

92   Site plan
          Site isometric from southeast

PROJECT CREDITS

Building: Ledbury Park
Architect: Shim-Sutcliffe Architects/
G+G Partnership Architects
Building address: 160 Ledbury Street, Toronto,
Ontario. Park entrance – Ledbury Street at
St. Germain Ave.
Location: Mid-block neighbourhood park, two
blocks east of Bathurst Street and two blocks
west of Avenue Road, eight blocks north of
Lawrence Avenue West
Client: Derek Nicholson – Director of Design
Services, City of North York, Parks and
Recreation Department

Architect team: Brigitte Shim, Howard Sutcliffe,
(Shim-Sutcliffe Architects); Girish Ghatalia, John
Greenan, Robert Goyeche, Ralph Beckmann,
Vlad Pavliuc (G+G Partnership Architects)
Structural: Banerjee Anderson and
Associates, Inc.
Mechanical & electrical: Rybka Smith
Ginsler Ltd.
Landscape: Robert Ng / NAK Design Group
Colour consultant: Margaret Priest – Fine
Artist
Water play fountain consultant: DanEuser
Waterarchitecture

General contractor: Carosi Construction
Swimming pool contractor: Acapulco Pools
Landscape contractor: City of North York,
Parks Construction Division
Pedestrian bridge fabricator: Eagle Bridge
Inc.
Weathering steel fountain fabricator:
Tremonte Manufacturing Ltd.
Custom light standards: Lumca
Budget: $2.5 million
Photography: James Dow, except page 90 and
lower left page 94, Steven Evans
Models: Richard Sinclair, John Featherstone

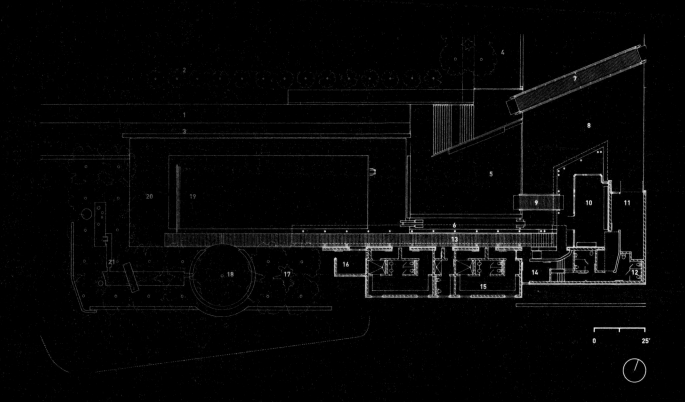

0   25'

Floor plan
1. Main pedestrian walkway 2. Row of pyramidal
oaks 3. Ornamental grasses 4. Alley of pleached
lindens 5. Plaza 6. Year round fountain, water
trough 7. Cor-ten steel pedestrian bridge
8. Skating canal / reflecting pool 9. Plaza bridge
10. View pavilion

11. Zamboni garage 12. Public washrooms
13. Boardwalk and trellis 14. Maintenance office
15. Change rooms 16. Lifeguard office 17. Grove of
honey locust trees 18. Children's wading pool
19. Swimming pool 20. Pool deck 21. Children's
water play

Medals for Merit / Médailles du mérite

National Archives of Canada

Revenue Canada Building

Pavillon de design de l'Université du Québec à Montréal

Rotary Park Pool

Cinémathèque québécoise

National Archives of Canada

Blouin IKOY & Associés

PROJECT DESCRIPTION: Sited on a suburban field that is part of a proposed civic centre for the town of Gatineau, just outside Ottawa, the great shed of the new archives building is inscribed within a huge ellipse drawn upon the landscape. This landscape device distinguishes the ordered, geometric construct of the archives from the naturalistic perimeter given over to marshes, woodland and meadows.

As a treasure chest of the nation's memory, the symbolism and the technical strategy of the archives all support a program that is, in the simplest possible terms, immortality. To this end, the massing and shaping produce a single-volume space with a curved metal roof that floats above the central concrete vaults of the archives and is supported by elaborate 25-metre stainless steel columns and beams that extend beyond the envelope to give the impression of a temple. Within this space are the central concrete vaults for the archives, surrounded on all sides by a fully controlled, artificial climate – a thermal neutral environment. The building's technology seeks to counteract the effects of osmosis, which has been the Achilles heel of conventional archives.

On top of the vaults is a "village" of interior buildings where archivists preserve and conserve archival products. Surrounding the vaults is a public gallery. The monochromatic silver underside of the roof is conceived as the sky of the archivists' village and the gallery, thereby creating a public dimension to the building where none had existed in the program. The sloping floor of the gallery enables archival material to pass below, from the shipping area to the archives. Below the vaults is a crawl space.

The concrete shell of the vaults tapers subtly as it rises, according to diminishing structural necessity. Beyond the vaults, additional layers accrue: the outer structure, with its stainless steel tension-compression columns; the highly impervious glass and metal skin; and finally, the mechanical elements contained in a scion outside the main envelope.

Every component and system in the building was considered in relation to its projected life span and ease of transformation. The primary structures – the stainless steel superstructure, the curved steel beams, and the cast-in-place concrete shell – have a projected life span of more than 500 years. The secondary structures – the piano stool-like columns and the painted steel cages supporting the elevators – are less permanent. Tertiary elements include stairs and handrails in stainless and ordinary steel, and the self-supporting structure of the archivists' village. Wall dividers in the village are either corrugated metal fixed to steel frames or prefabricated melamine sandwich panels that, unlike drywall, create no dust and can be reconfigured easily if future modifications are required.

JURY COMMENT: "The National Archives of Canada is set in a particularly unattractive no-man's-land of shopping malls, industrial parks, and suburban housing. The challenge for Blouin IKOY & Associés was surely daunting: how to make and place an enormous storage warehouse (more eloquently referred to by the architects as 'a treasure chest for the nation's memory') on this ugly landscape. What they did – a glass shed arching over concrete storage vaults – is striking. Not only is it a state-of-the-art facility in terms of international archive standards; more importantly, it is an inventive 'village' for the people who work there. Within, one finds a silvery presence of crazy columns supporting a softly arching roof that embraces a convincing distribution of programme elements. Much less convincing is the weak shaping of the land and the spindly planting that surrounds the building, smacking of a stingy landscape budget. One can only hope that funds will be found to complete this park in a manner that is up to the level of the building itself. Otherwise, any notion of this becoming a key part of a new Gatineau 'civic centre' of any real quality seems unlikely." **Larry Richards**

PROJECT CREDITS
Building: National Archives of Canada
Architect: Blouin IKOY & Associés
Building address: 625 boulevard du Carrefour, Gatineau, Québec
Location: west of rue Paiement, north of boulevard Greber
Client: National Archives of Canada, Department of Public Works (Derek Ballantyne & Dr. Lily Koltun, Director General, Archives Headquarters Accommodation Project)
Architect team: Ron Keenberg, with Paul Faucher, Dominique McEwen, Don Blakey, Hein Hulsbosch, Magda Hulsbosch, Paul Bernier, Lee McCormick
Structural: Nicolet Chartrand Knoll
Mechanical & electrical: ECE Group
Building envelope: Morrison Hershfield
Landscape: Hilderman Witty Crosby Hanna
Contractor: Hervé Pomerleau Inc. & PCL Construction Western Inc.
Budget: $68.7 million
Photography: Steven Evans

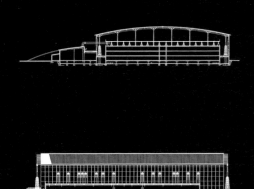

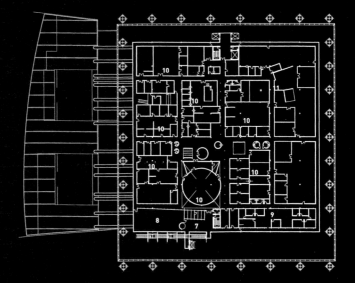

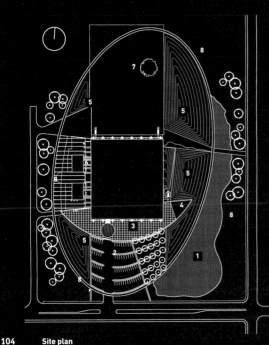

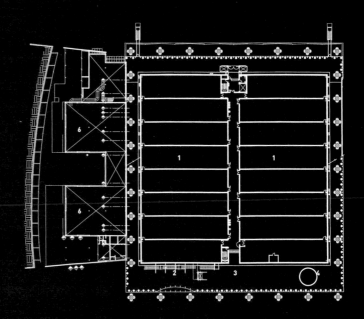

Site plan
1. Pond 2. Parking / drive-in movie theatre 3. Entry
court 4. Food court 5. Berm covered with sumac
6. Mechanical service 7. Grassed courts 8. Wood lot
and meadow

Top floor plan
Ground floor plan
1. Archives 2. Entrance lobby 3. Theatre / reception
area 4. Eating area 5. Public display gallery
6. Mechanical / electrical room 7. Lobby 8. Library
9. Administration 10. Laboratories 11. Records

Revenue Canada Building

Busby + Associates Architects

PROJECT DESCRIPTION: The Revenue Canada Building is a response to a design/ build competition with an emphasis on low life-cycle costs. Hundreds of aspects of this 11,150 m^2 office building were carefully examined to maintain green design principles while staying within the $16.9 million budget.

Because staff work teams in the building are expected to be relocated every month, flexibility is crucial. The 95%-efficient floor plate maximizes the available floor area, while the internal dimensions guarantee that almost all workstations are no more than eight metres from natural light and operable windows. The key to flexibility is an accessible raised floor system with flush floor monuments for distributing air, power and communications from below. 100% fresh air is provided in large volume at low velocity, and employees can control the location and velocity of supply air at each workstation. The pressurized floor plenum is easy to clean and contains almost no ducts to harbour dirt and environmental contaminants. The added cost of the raised floor system was offset by savings elsewhere in the building due to smaller mechanical systems, a more efficient structure, elimination of dropped ceilings, and a lower overall building height.

Exterior sunscreens, internal light shelves, and low-E glazing provide a very energy-efficient envelope. To avoid glare in this highly computerized environment, suspended indirect lighting provides 70% uplight and 30% downlight. The curved glass sunshades filter direct solar gain, minimize glare on computer screens, and provide deep daylight penetration toward the core of the building, reducing the reliance on artificial light. Photo

sensors optimize internal lighting conditions automatically, with significant energy savings. Operable windows and cross-ventilation also reduce energy loads in shoulder seasons. The absence of dropped ceilings allows heat from occupants and equipment to be absorbed during the day by the thermal mass of the exposed concrete ceilings, then purged during evening hours. This dynamic thermal storage enabled the building's mechanical equipment to be reduced in size, with lower maintenance costs. The building operates at 60–70% below the targetted ASHRAE 90.1 compliance.

The building has a simple, five-storey concrete structure, with glazing, cladding and a brick base that were considered appropriate for a government building. The low-rise, stepped massing was chosen for urban design considerations and for reasons of cost and energy efficiency. The building is sited to define a continuous street edge along King George Highway and to provide a new "front door" to the larger site, which includes an existing office building. Existing mature plane trees filter natural light entering the building, while additional landscaping and exterior features define the entry plaza and an outdoor area that serves as a lunch-hour staff retreat. Through resourcefulness, innovation, and attention to long-term operation, this building demonstrates that green design principles are compatible with a limited budget.

JURY COMMENT: "This is a modest building taking on one of architecture's significant agendas. It forms itself carefully according to a limited budget and a set of environmental concerns. Its results are at certain moments remarkably successful, producing in the general office areas on the upper floors lofty, light filled spaces with fresh air from operable windows and associated views of the central landscape court." **Patricia Patkau**

PROJECT CREDITS

Building: Revenue Canada Building
Architect: Busby + Associates Architects
Building address: 9755 King George Highway, Surrey, BC
Location: north of 96 Avenue
Client: Public Works and Government Services Canada
Architect team: Peter Busby, Stephan Chevalier, Joanne Heinen, Jim Huffman, Michael McColl (associate-in-charge), Susan Ockwell, Alfred Waugh, Sören Schou, Clive Eveleigh

Structural: Jones Kwong Kishi
Mechanical: Keen Engineering Co. Ltd.
Electrical: Reid Crowther & Partners
Landscape: Site Design Solutions
Acoustical: Barron Kennedy Lyzun + Associates
Fire code: Protection Engineering Inc.
Development advisors: Mitchell Kime Thompson Inc.
Contractor: Ledcor Industries Ltd.
Budget: $16.9 million
Photography: Martin Tessler

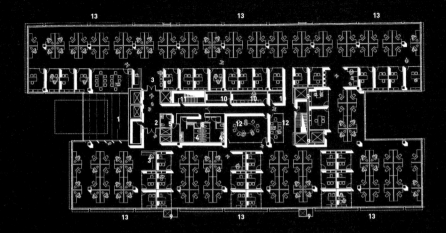

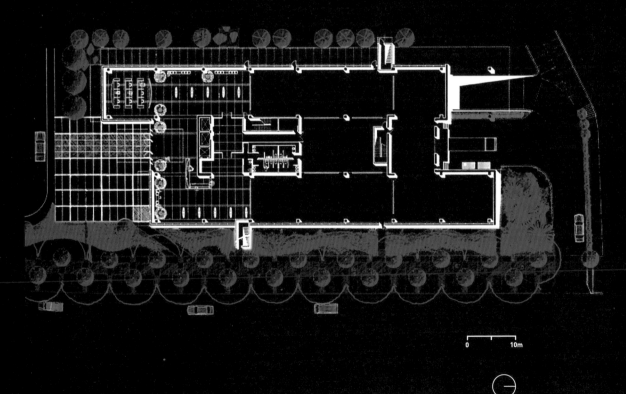

0   10m

112   **Typical floor plan**
Ground floor plan
1. Open to below 2. Elevator lobby 3. Reception /
waiting area 4. Employee washrooms 5. Disabled
washroom 6. Data room 7. Electrical room
8. Janitor room 9. Mechanical shaft 10. Storage
11. Exit stair 12. Meeting room 13. Sunshade

Pavillon de design de l'Université du Québec à Montréal

Dan S. Hanganu, Architects

LE PROJET : Relié par un tunnel au campus principal et au métro, le Pavillon de design s'insère fièrement dans son cadre urbain. Le bâtiment, qui construit l'îlot Sanguinet, de Boisbriand, Sainte-Élisabeth et Sainte-Catherine, se compose de deux équerres emboîtées à l'intérieur desquelles se niche une cour-jardin qui participe à ce dialogue avec la ville et l'environnement. L'organisation logique de l'immeuble veut que chaque regroupement fonctionnel soit reconnaissable à la fois de l'intérieur et de l'extérieur.

De la place UQÀM, en face, l'entrée et son parvis, rue Sanguinet, découvrent l'activité commerciale et culturelle du rez-de-chaussée. Les aires de circulation deviennent zones d'échanges. La galerie intérieure demeure le lieu privilégié qui incarne l'identité même du pavillon. Éclairée naturellement, elle oriente le déplacement depuis le foyer d'entrée, suivi de la salle d'exposition, jusqu'au toit-terrasse.

Du foyer, un grand escalier mène au "piano nobile," où siège l'administration. Les salles de classe sont regroupées sur deux niveaux à l'extrémité ouest du bâtiment, facilement accessible depuis le métro. Aux étages supérieurs, deux niveaux d'ateliers de production sont en relation avec les classes, les bureaux de professeurs et la cafétéria. Ils forment le noyau de l'activité interne de l'école. Au dernier étage, le centre de documentation et les laboratoires informatiques campent aux deux angles importants du bâtiment.

Les ateliers multitechniques logeant au premier sous-sol, dans un espace à double hauteur largement fenestré, à l'angle des rues Sainte-Elisabeth et de Boisbriand, offrent aux passants des vues plongeantes jusque dans les entrailles de l'édifice.

Rue Sanguinet, le Pavillon de design illustre ses caractéristiques spatiales internes, notamment par la galerie intérieure qui divise le bâtiment en deux. D'un côté, les ateliers de production sont exprimés en élévation dans un volume presque opaque au-dessus d'une colonnade de deux étages dégageant le parvis de l'entrée principale et le volume circulaire de la salle d'observation. En surplomb, l'œuvre de Pierre E. Leclerc, tel un grand panneau d'affichage, signale le caractère à la fois ludique et rigoureux de l'établissement. De l'autre côté, un escalier, entièrement vitré, assure la liaison visuelle entre le bâtiment principal et l'aile plus basse réservée au corps professoral, tout en marquant le retournement en équerre vers la cour intérieure.

En tant qu'outil pédagogique, le Pavillon de design fait le pont entre l'intention architecturale et la solution construite. Pour ce projet de 10 000 m2 réalisé au coût de 1180 $/m², l'emploi inédit de matériaux modestes et la composition spatiale modulée par la lumière ont orienté le travail. Toutes les composantes techniques, dévoilées au grand jour, contribuent ici à l'expression de la forme architecturale.

JURY COMMENT: "Le pavillon contribue de façon remarquable au travail d'intégration à la ville que poursuit l'UQAM depuis sa création (mais dont la qualité architecturale est pour le moins variable). Ce projet brut, sculptural et lumineux tire parti d'un site biscornu et en retrait des artères principales et réussit à donner au Pavillon une adresse publique marquée et à consolider le rôle de catalyseur du centre de design qu'il abrite. L'organisation des espaces de part et d'autre d'une grande faille éclairée et conviviale, menant du parvis jusqu'à la terrasse sur le toit, contribue à la consolidation de l'identité de l'école et au succès du projet. Un bémol: les grands ateliers de fabrication qui sont un important témoins de l'activitée du département sont situés à l'écart de l'ensemble."
Anne Cormier

PROJECT CREDITS

Building: Pavillon de design, Université du Québec à Montréal
Architect: Dan S. Hanganu, Architects
Building address: 1440 rue Sanguinet, Montréal, QC
Location: north of rue Ste.-Catherine, one block west of rue St.-Denis
Client: Université du Québec à Montréal
Architect team: Dan S. Hanganu (principal-in-charge), Gilles Prud'homme, Guillaume de Lorimier (project architects), Earl Murphy, Rose-Marie Tariant, François Poirier, Marie-Danielle Faucher, Andrew Zygal, Alex Touikan, Viorel Indries, Radu C. Jean
Structural: Boulva, Kadanoff, Saia, Deslauriers
Mechanical & electrical: Pellemon Inc.
Contractor: Pisapia Ltée
Budget: $13.5 million
Photography: Michel Brunelle

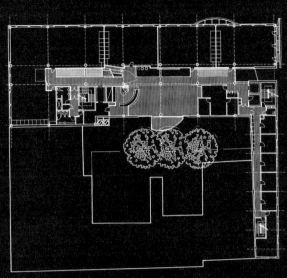

3ième étage

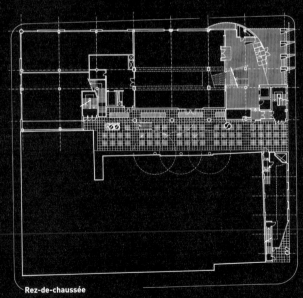

Rez-de-chaussée

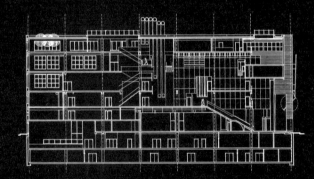

0   10m

118   **3ième étage**
1. Atelier de production 2. Café 3. Balcon 4. Bureau
de professeur 5. Vide

Rez-de-chaussée
1. Parvis 2. Hall 3. Salle d'exposition 4. Dépot

6ième étage
1. Classe d'informatique 2. Centre de
documentation 3. Bureau de professeur
4. Bureau de recherche 5. Terrasse 6. Vide

Longitudinal section

Rotary Park Pool

MacLennan Jaunkalns Miller Architects Limited

PROJECT DESCRIPTION: Rotary Park is one of several small waterfront parks in Etobicoke, west of Toronto. Each is surrounded by a residential area and supports a municipal recreation building. In Rotary Park there is an open, buildable area to the north and a lower area with unstable fill and mature trees that extends south to Lake Ontario.

The program was to demolish an existing 1960s in-ground swimming pool and to construct a new 400 m^2 pool pavilion and a series of new pools, including 25 m training lanes, shallow children's areas and a splash pad. The facility contains family, men's and women's change facilities, as well as an open public lobby and viewing area. It is intended for seasonal use.

The building is located at the north end of the site to support the heavy pool volume on stable soil, to minimize excavation, and to maintain the mature willows and elms to the south. A conservation strategy to protect existing trees determined the location of excavation areas and walls.

The pavilion is extended along 11th Street, with an open glazed lobby and a breezeway covered by a continuous sloped roof. A viewing gallery shaded by a pergola enables parents to supervise their children in the pools and to overlook the playgrounds in the wooded area to the south. Security and visibility were major concerns expressed during the community design process. The building is intentionally transparent, with a sliding wooden screen to protect the glazed area during the winter.

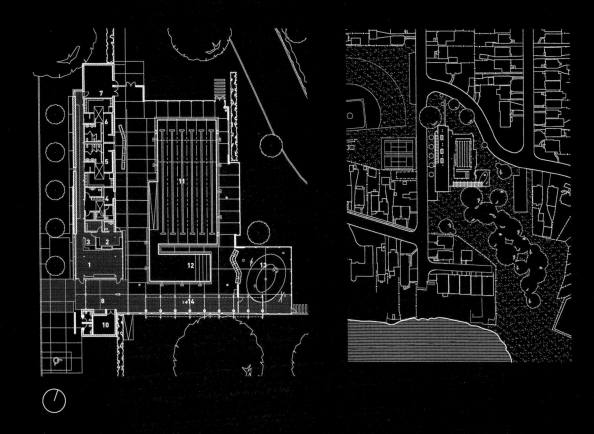

124   **Floor plan**
1. Lobby 2. Office 3. Reception 4. Family change area 5. Female change room 6. Male change room 7. Pool mechanical 8. Vestibule 9. Washroom 10. Pool storage 11. 25m lap pool 12. Wading pool 13. Splash pad 14. Viewing area under pergola

Site plan

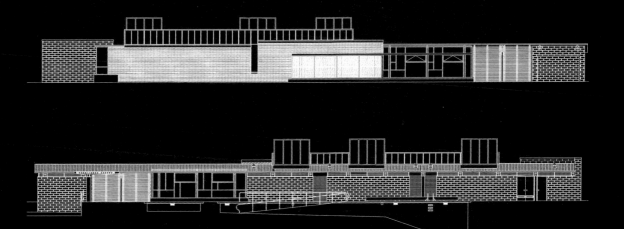

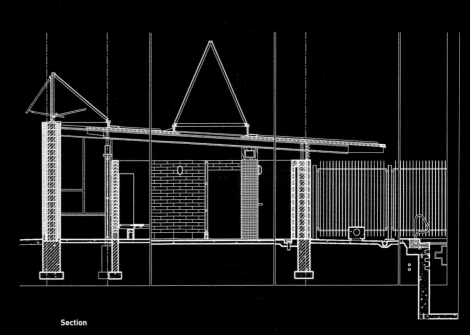

West elevation
East elevation

Section

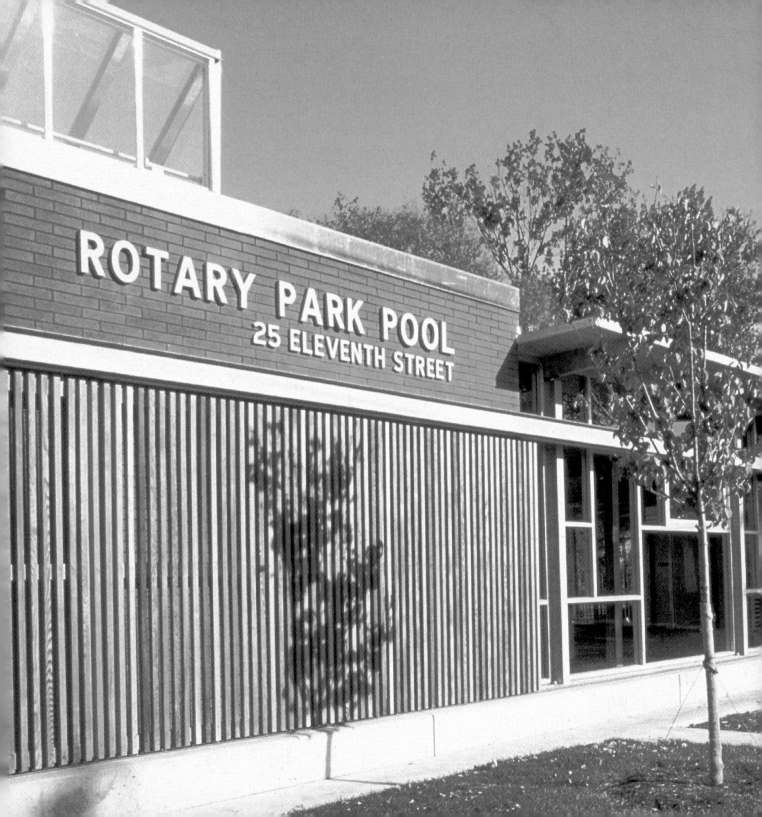

To minimize the use of mechanical and electrical systems, the building was designed for natural flow-through ventilation, using large pivoting greenhouse glazing to the prevailing winds and continuous louvres to the east. The interior walls are only 2.4 m high to ensure air circulation. The building is skylit in all major public areas to eliminate the need for lighting during the day. The main public corridor has a continuous ridge skylight with operable panels, and the change rooms have large peaked skylights. The pool water is recirculated to the wading pool to centralize the filtration system. Rainwater from the roof overhang drips directly into a linear deck drain that is scuppered into the lower park area. This minimizes the run-off water directed into the storm drainage system.

The reduction of public funding for municipal projects has resulted in a palette of robust materials that are economical and simple to construct, and low in maintenance. The structure of the building is a galvanized steel frame with wood beams and decking. The perimeter walls are pigmented concrete block, with a brick wall along the front of the building, facing west. The floor is polished concrete with a ceramic tile finish in the shower areas. The skylights and lobby windows are single-glazed greenhouse sections.

JURY COMMENT: "Rotary Park Pool succeeds as a truly indoor/outdoor space. Boundaries that appear solid are in fact guiding elements that bring one from the street to the pool, through an orchestrated changing sequence. The architects recognized the opportunities afforded by the seasonal nature of the building and took every advantage to create a delicately detailed structure. Clever use of greenhouse technology allows the indoor space to transform into an outdoor space in summer. The pool has a controlled, yet playful quality that makes it a fulfilling destination of this sequence." **Stephen Teeple**

PROJECT CREDITS
Building: Rotary Park Pool
Architect: MacLennan Jaunkalns Miller Architects Limited
Building address: 11th Street and Lakeshore Drive, Etobicoke, Ontario
Location: on Lake Ontario, south of Queen Elizabeth Way and Islington Avenue
Client: City of Toronto, Parks and Recreation Division (Susan Korrick, Capital Construction/Renovation Co-ordinator)
Architect team: Robert Allen, Lou Ampas, Lisa D'Abbondanza, Viktors Jaunkalns, Edmund Lee, John MacLennan, Drew Mandel, David Miller, Carol Phillips, Maia Puccetti, Blair Robinson, Ted Watson

Structural: Blackwell Engineering
Mechanical & Electrical: Day and Behn
Landscape: Gunta Mackars Landscape Architecture
Contractor: Melloul-Blamey Construction
Public art installation (benches, p. 129 upper right): Carol Phillips, Jarle Lovlin, Robin Greenwood; commissioned by Public Arts Committee, City of Toronto
Budget: $1.6 million
Photography: Richard Seck Associates (p. 123, p. 129 lower right; MacLennan Jaunkalns Miller Architects Ltd. (all other photos)

129

Cinémathèque québécoise

Saucier + Perrotte architectes

PROJECT DESCRIPTION: The Cinémathèque québécoise is a new cultural focus in the heart of Montreal. It has been realized in large part by adapting a former school and an adjacent two-storey brick building. The school has been replanned to house public spaces at street level with administrative offices above. Externally, its ornate brick and stone facade has been retained but the interior spaces radically reorganized to accommodate foyers, a shop and a new 175–seat cinema. Classrooms, offices, studios and exhibition areas for the film school have been skilfully fitted into the other building.

The character of the cinémathèque is most emphatically established by a new building within the slot of space between these two existing structures. A new connecting link across the back of the site houses a café, a small cinema and exhibition gallery. This connection also frames an outdoor dining terrace which is directly accessible from both café and street and creates a site for a new light box.

As the word light refers to conditions of weight and illumination, so the design of this box explores both qualities within the context of the moving image. In describing the differences between a photograph and the moving image, Susan Sontag has noted how "movies and television programs light up walls, flicker and go out" (*On Photography*, 1979, p. 3). These aspects of movement and changing light qualities have clearly informed the design of the new light box and the organization of the cinémathèque.

The light box is the main entrance to the building. A gridded glass screen projects out over the doors of the entry lobby and also extends beyond the box as a conspicuous layer

drawn across the restored brick and stone facade. A piece of this glazed skin is a translu-
cent screen which is used to project moving images that can be viewed from the street.
A ramped *passerelle* between projector and screen permits the silhouetted images of
people moving within the building to appear periodically on the screen.

In sharp contrast to the widely assumed notion of the cinema as a sealed black box,
the light entrance hall also acts as a cinema. A second screen, suspended opposite the
entrance, confronts the visitor on entering and a raked canopy over the entrance lobby is
also a balcony for 50 people. This space blurs the distinction between observer and
observed in ways which the traditionally dark and enclosed cinema rarely achieves.

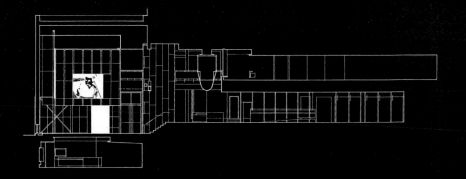

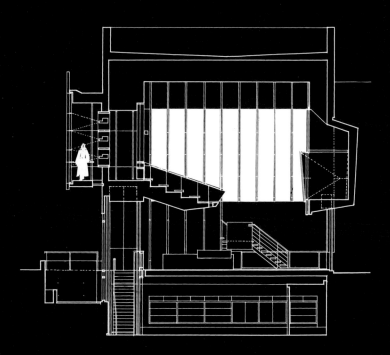

PROJECT CREDITS
Building: Cinémathèque québécoise
Architect: Saucier + Perrotte architectes
Building address: 335 boulevard de Maisonneuve est, Montreal, QC
Location: one block west of rue St.-Denis
Client: Cinémathèque québécoise
Architect team: Gilles Saucier, André Perrotte, Robert D'Errico, Martin Bouchard, Andrew Dunbar, Franck Thonon, Jean-François Lagacé, Lyse Lachance, Oscar Juarros, Pierre Colpron
Structural: Teknica Inc.
Mechanical & electrical: Teknika Inc./Dupras Ledoux
Interiors: Saucier + Perrotte architectes
Landscape: Saucier + Perrotte architectes
Budget: $8.15 million
Photography: Eric Piché; except p. 135 upper right: Marc-Antoine Daudelin

Longitudianl section
Cross section

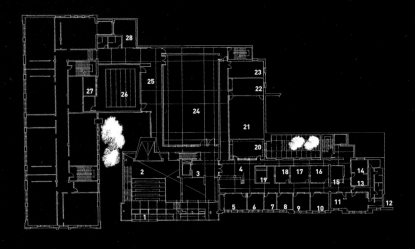

Second floor plan

0   5m

Ground floor plan

0   5m

Ground floor plan

1. Vestibule 2. Hall 3. Cloakroom 4. Exhibition gallery 5. Shop 6. Director 7. Accounting 8. Deputy director 9. Messenger 10. Communications 11. Projection room 12. Storage 13. Claude-Jutra theatre 14. Exhibition room 15. Café 16. Terrace / garden 17. Kitchen 18. Loading docks 19. Parking 20. Multimedia showcases

Second floor plan

1. Catwalk (on facade) 2. Suspended agora 3. Hall 4. Reception 5. Acquisitions 6. Coordination 7. Technical exhibition 8. Animation curator 9. Quebec cinema curator 10. Conservation curator 11. Break room 12. Kitchen 13. Film collection technician 14. Film collection administration 15. Small video room 16. Television curator

17. Non-film conservation curator 18. Indexation 19. Office furniture 20. Meeting room / video room 21. Photo storage / paper archives 22. Non-film collection administration 23. Technical and computers 24. Exhibition room / permanent collection 25. Foyer 26. Projection room / video 27. Technical projection room 28. Storage

A series of glass and steel layers filter light, a fragment of the concrete frame of the existing school is suddenly exposed, and the palette of materials within these internal spaces is monochromatic. The tones of black and grey, together with the lustre and grain of surfaces, exemplify Sontag's sense of film.

The design of this building creates and frames a series of passing glimpses which combine activity and artifacts, old buildings and new light box, actor and audience, street and room – fleeting images which are tantalizingly projected, through architecture, into the life and spaces of the city.

– Brian Carter, *Architectural Review*, Aug. 1998

JURY COMMENT: "This project is an exceptional collusion of Saucier + Perrotte's design sensibilities, with an evocative program and a very appropriate site. A filmic spatial experience is implied as one transgresses boundaries, moving in and out of the picture, from stage to audience, through thin layers of space. New construction slides seamlessly into the existing structure, creating an exquisite place of celebration. It is a building composed of intermittent, syncopated light and darkness. The cinematic metaphors and spatial parallels are never overbearing. Each theatre space is carefully conceived and created, as are the indoor and outdoor public rooms." **Stephen Teeple**

Critic

Wilfried Wang was born in Hamburg and studied architecture in London. He has written essays and monographs on architecture, and is a co-editor of *9H*, with Rosamund Diamond, Marcel Meili and Linda Pollak. From 1986 to 1989 he was assistant professor of architecture at Harvard University Graduate School of Design and is currently adjunct professor of architecture there. From 1989 to 1995 he was a partner with John Southall in SW Architects Ltd. From 1995 to 2000 he served as the director at the German Architecture Museum in Frankfurt am Main, and is currently practising in Berlin.

The Jury

Anne Cormier is one of three architectural practitioners who comprise Atelier Big City in Montreal. All are active researchers and teachers as well. Recognized for its unique approach to design and building, the collective has demonstrated its interest in the urban environment and its concern for the public dimension of architecture. Atelier Big City has received two Awards for Merit in the Governor General's Awards for Architecture competition (1994 and 1997). In 1998 the collective won the Canada Council Prix de Rome in Architecture. Ms. Cormier received her B.Sc.(Arch.) and B.Arch. from McGill University before attending École d'architecture Paris-Villemin from 1985 to 1987.

Susan A. Maxman, FAIA, Hon. FRAIC, has been the principal of her own firm in Philadelphia since 1980. She is a graduate of Smith College (class of 1960), and received her Master of Architecture from the University of Pennsylvania in 1977. In 1993 Ms. Maxman became the first female president of the American Institute of Architects. Currently, she serves as Assistant Chair of the Urban Land Institute's Environmental Council. For her advocacy of sustainable design, Ms. Maxman has received honorary doctorates from Ball State University and the University of Detroit-Mercy. As well as being admitted to the College of Fellows of the AIA, Ms. Maxman is an Honorary Fellow of the Royal Architectural Institute of Canada.

Patricia Patkau, FRAIC, received her Bachelor of Interior Design degree from the University of Manitoba and a Master of Architecture from Yale University. Ms. Patkau is an active practitioner and teacher, and has served as a juror in many national and international competitions. The firm, Patkau Architects Inc., has been the recipient of two Awards for Merit and four Medals for Excellence in the Governor General's Awards for Architecture competition. Exhibitions of the firm's work have been displayed worldwide, including the Venice Biennale. Ms. Patkau was made a Fellow of the Royal Architectural Institute of Canada in 1993/94, and is an Honorary Fellow of the American Institute of Architects.

Gino Pin, FRAIC, has practiced architecture in the Northwest Territories for 26 years and formed his current firm, Pin/Matthews Architects, in 1987. Through the years, Mr. Pin has developed a sensitivity to the special requirements of the northern landscape and climate. The cultural needs of the First Nations are addressed through extensive consultation and incorporation of traditional symbols and materials. His philosophy is to make architecture work with the arctic conditions, not against them. Mr. Pin received his Bachelor of Architecture from the Nova Scotia Technical College in 1965, and was made a Fellow of the Royal Architectural Institute of Canada in 1986.

Larry Wayne Richards, FRAIC, is Dean of the Faculty of Architecture, Landscape, and Design at the University of Toronto. During the 1960s he worked with Walter Gropius and The Architects Collaborative, then completed a Master of Architecture at Yale University. In 1975 he immigrated to Halifax to teach at the Nova Scotia Technical College and was a member of the group NETWORKS. He served as Director of the University of Waterloo School of Architecture from 1982 to 1987. Mr. Richards was editor of the book *Canadian Centre for Architecture: Building and Gardens*, and has published numerous articles on contemporary architecture and design. In 1999 he was made a Fellow of the Royal Architectural Institute of Canada.

Stephen Teeple, FRAIC, is the principal of his Toronto-based firm, established in 1989. He is currently a fifth year thesis adjunct professor at the University of Toronto. His firm has become known for designing both large and small scale institutional buildings with a strong conceptual basis derived from the specific needs and aspirations of each client. The firm has been the recipient of two Awards for Merit in the Governor General's Awards for Architecture competition (1994 and 1997). Mr. Teeple received his Bachelor of Environmental Studies and Bachelor of Architecture degrees from the University of Waterloo, and a Master of Science (B.D.) from Columbia University. He was made a Fellow of the Royal Architectural Institute of Canada in 1998.

Critique

Wilfried Wang est né à Hamburg et a étudié l'architecture à Londres. Auteur d'articles et de monographies sur l'architecture, il a publié *9H* avec Rosamund Diamond, Marcel Meili et Linda Pollak. De 1986 à 1989, il a été professeur adjoint d'architecture à l'école d'études supérieures en design de l'Université Harvard où il est actuellement professeur associé. De 1989 à 1995, il a fait équipe avec John Southall chez SW Architects Ltd. De 1995 à 2000, il a dirigé le Musée d'architecture allemande à Frankfurt sur le Main. Il exerce actuellement à Berlin.

Les Jurés

Anne Cormier est l'une des trois architectes, doublés de chercheurs et d'enseignants actifs, qui forment l'Atelier Big City à Montréal. Réputé pour son approche unique du design et du bâti, le groupe a montré qu'il s'intéressait à l'environnement bâti et se préoccupait de la dimension publique de l'architecture. L'Atelier Big City a reçu deux Médailles du mérite à l'occasion des concours des Prix du Gouverneur général pour l'architecture de 1994 et 1997. En 1998, le groupe a remporté le Prix de Rome en architecture du Conseil des arts du Canada. Mme Cormier est titulaire d'un B.Sc.Arch. et d'un B.Arch., de l'Université McGill et a fréquenté l'École d'architecture Paris-Villemin de 1985 à 1987.

Susan A. Maxman, FAIA, Hon. FRAIC, dirige sa propre firme à Philadephie (Pennsylvanie) depuis 1980. Diplômée du Smith College en 1960, elle a obtenu sa maîtrise en architecture de l'Université de Pennsylvanie en 1977. En 1993, Mme Maxman fut la première femme à accéder à la présidence du American Institute of Architects. Actuellement, elle est co-présidente du conseil de l'environnement du Urban Land Institute. Son plaidoyer inlassable pour le design durable lui a valu des doctorats honorifiques des universités Ball State et de Detroit-Mercy. Membre du Collège of Fellows de l'AIA, Mme Maxman est aussi fellow honoraire de l'Institut royal d'architecture du Canada.

Patricia Patkau, FRAIC, détient un baccalauréat en design intérieur de l'Université du Manitoba et une maîtrise en architecture de l'Université Yale. Professionnelle en exercice et enseignante active, elle a fait partie du jury de nombreux concours nationaux et internationaux. La firme Patkau Architects Inc. a obtenu deux Médailles du mérite et quatre Médailles d'excellence lors de concours des prix du Gouverneur général pour l'architecture. Les travaux de la firme ont été exposés dans le monde entier, notamment à la biennale de Venise. Mme Patkau est devenue fellow de l'Institut royal d'architecture du Canada en 1993–1994 et est fellow honoraire de l'American Institute of Architects.

Gino Pin, FRAIC, pratique l'architecture dans les Territoires du Nord-Ouest depuis 26 ans et a constitué sa firme actuelle, Pin/Matthews Architects, en 1987. Au fil des ans, M. Pin a appris à apprécier les exigences spéciales du paysage et du climat du Nord. Pour répondre aux besoins culturels des Premières nations, il effectue de vastes consultations et incorpore les symboles et matériaux traditionnels. Sa philosophie est de marier l'architecture et les conditions arctiques et non pas de les opposer. M. Pin a obtenu son baccalauréat en architecture de la Technical University of Nova Scotia en 1965 et est devenu fellow de l'Institut royal d'architecture du Canada en 1986.

Larry Wayne Richards, FRAIC, est doyen de la faculté d'architecture, d'aménagement paysager et de design de l'Université de Toronto. Pendant les années 60, il a travaillé avec Walter Gropius et The Architects Collaborative, puis a obtenu sa maîtrise en architecture à l'Université Yale. En 1975, il a déménagé à Halifax pour enseigner au Nova Scotia Technical College et a fait partie du groupe NETWORKS. Il a été directeur de l'école d'architecture de Waterloo de 1982 à 1987. M. Richards a édité le livre *Canadian Centre for Architecture: Building and Gardens* et a publié de nombreux articles sur l'architecture et le design contemporains. En 1999, il a reçu le titre de fellow de l'Institut royal d'architecture du Canada.

Stephen Teeple, FRAIC, dirige sa firme établie à Toronto en 1989. Il est actuellement professeur adjoint en cinquième année de préparation de thèse à l'Université de Toronto. Son bureau s'est distingué en concevant de petits et grands édifices publics dont le concept s'inspire largement des besoins et des aspirations de chaque client. L'entreprise a reçu deux Médailles du mérite à l'occasion des concours des Prix du Gouverneur général pour l'architecture de 1994 et 1997. M. Teeple a obtenu son baccalauréat en études environnementales et son baccalauréat en architecture de l'Université de Waterloo et une maîtrise ès sciences (B.D.) de l'Université Columbia. Il est devenu fellow de l'Institut royal d'architecture du Canada en 1998.

Firms / Les architectes

Blouin IKOY et Associés
325 Dalhousie, Street, #903
Ottawa, Ontario
K1N 7G2

Busby + Associates Architects
1050 Homer Street
Vancouver, British Columbia
V6B 2W9

Peter Cardew Architects
1661 Duranleau Street
Vancouver, British Columbia
V6H 3S3

Dan S. Hanganu Architectes
404, rue Saint-Dizier
Montréal, Québec
H2Y 3T3

Julien Architectes et
Les architectes Plante et Julien
203, avenue Laurier ouest
Montréal, Québec
H2T 2N9

Levitt Goodman Architects
533 College Street, Suite 404
Toronto, Ontario
M6G 1A8

MacLennan Jaunkalns Miller Architects
19 Duncan Street, Suite 202
Toronto, Ontario
M5H 3H1

Saia et Barbarese Architectes
339, rue St-Paul est, 3ième étage
Montréal, Québec
H2Y 3T3

Saucier + Perrotte architectes
5334, boulevard St-Laurent
Montréal, Québec
H2T 1S1

Shim-Sutcliffe Architects
441 Queen Street East
Toronto, Ontario
M5A 1T5

Other publications by Tuns Press:
Barry Johns Architects: Selected Projects 1984–1998,
ISBN 0-929112-32-6, 2000
Urban Structure — Halifax: An Urban Design Approach,
ISBN 0-929112-42-3, 1998
Brian MacKay-Lyons: Selected Projects 1986–1997,
ISBN 0-929112-39-3, 1998
Architecture Canada 1997: The Governor General's Awards for Architecture,
ISBN 0-929112-38-5, 1997
Works: The Architecture of A.J. Diamond, Donald Schmitt & Company,
ISBN 0-929112-31-8, 1996
Patkau Architects: Selected Projects 1983–1993,
ISBN 0-929112-28-8, 1994
A Pictorial History of St. Paul's Anglican Church, Halifax, Nova Scotia,
ISBN 0-929112-19-9, 1993